Southern Literary Studies
Louis D. Rubin, Jr., Editor

LITERARY NEW ORLEANS

LITERARY NEW ORLEANS
Essays and Meditations

EDITED BY
RICHARD S. KENNEDY

Louisiana State University Press   Baton Rouge

Copyright © 1992 by Louisiana State University Press
All rights reserved
Manufactured in the United States of America
Louisiana Paperback Edition, 1998
07 06 05 04 03 02 01 00 99 98   5 4 3 2 1

Designer: Amanda McDonald Key
Typeface: Sabon
Typesetter: G&S Typesetters, Inc.
Printer and binder: Thomson-Shore, Inc.

Library of Congress Cataloging-in-Publication Data

Literary New Orleans : essays and meditations / edited by Richard S.
    Kennedy.
        p.   cm. — (Southern literary studies)
    ISBN 0-8071-1732-3 (cloth)   ISBN 0-8071-2273-4 (pbk.)
        1. American literature—Louisiana—New Orleans—History and
criticism.   2. New Orleans (La.)—Intellectual life.   3. New Orleans
(La.) in literature.   I. Kennedy, Richard S.   II. Series.
    PS267.N49L58   1992
    810.9'976335—dc20   91-40564
                                                                CIP

Frontispiece photograph by Eugene Delacroix, courtesy of the State Library of Louisiana

The paper in this book meets the guidelines for permanence and durability of the Committee on
Production Guidelines for Book Longevity of the Council on Library Resources. ∞

For
Rayburn Moore and Mary Ann Wimsatt,
      Society for the Study of Southern Literature

CONTENTS

ILLUSTRATIONS

PREFACE

One day some years ago, while I was spending a summer in Concord, Massachusetts, I wandered into the Concord Public Library. The books were arranged, as usual, in categories—Fiction, Drama, Travel, Cookbooks, and so on. But there was one large section that bore the modest label Local Authors. Here were gathered the works of Emerson, Thoreau, Hawthorne, W. H. Channing, Bronson Alcott, Louisa May Alcott, and even Margaret Fuller. I was intrigued by the thought, What brought about such a literary efflorescence in this quiet New England village? Emerson, of course, was the magnet that drew most of the writers, although Thoreau happened to be born there.

The presence of a single stimulating figure has at times seemed the chief reason for a brief development of literary activity in other American communities. One thinks of John Crowe Ransom as the presiding genius for the Fugitive Group in Nashville in the 1920s and Allen Ginsberg as the guru of the Beat Generation in San Francisco during the 1950s. But when the central figure departed, the literary fires sank to embers.

A promising upsurge of literary vigor developed in Chicago in the teens and twenties of this century without any dominant figure. It is true that Sherwood Anderson was very briefly a mentor to the young Hemingway there, but Sandburg, Masters, Lindsay, Ben Hecht, and Floyd Dell worked independently—and soon all had gone to other cities, most of them to New York, which had already lured away two of Chicago's important literary magazines, the *Dial* and the *Little Review*.

When we ponder the question, What cities in the United States have served as genuine literary centers for any extensive period? we realize that Boston in the nineteenth century and New York in the twentieth are the only two places we can single out. Concord is really a satellite of Boston. Indeed, it is not a single powerful literary personality that is essential to the development of a literary center but rather the combination of a number of elements, among them: recurring periods of economic prosperity; a large population that includes the presence of a great many educated, literate citizens; a cultural context comprising a rich mix of theater, music, painting, sculpture, and the decorative arts; and the flourishing of magazine and book publication.

But Boston and New York differed in the combination of elements that spurred literary activity. In the Boston area, the intellectual vigor of Harvard College and the liberal nature of the Unitarian churches were distinct stimuli to literary creativity. Emerson, Thoreau, Prescott, Parkman, Motley, Lowell, Holmes, Dana, Higginson, and Adams were all Harvard graduates. Longfellow, Lowell, Ticknor, Sparks, and Adams were Harvard professors. Emerson, Channing, Parker, and Everett were Unitarian ministers.

In New York, however, the influence of the colleges and the churches does not appear evident. What seems more important is that New York had become the greatest trading center of the nation, which made possible not only the boom in publishing and the rise of the city as a great arts center but also the growth of an ethnically diverse population that brought in its wake a flow of European cultural influences.

But beyond these two northern cities, one other place that has been the focus of literary work for over a century cannot be ignored. The experience of New Orleans, although it was very unlike that of the northern American cities I have mentioned, has continued to provide an inspiration for literary creativity. Curiously enough, literature did not flourish during the flush times of the pre–Civil War period, when New Orleans, as the terminus of the river commerce of the nation and the gateway to Caribbean, Latin American, and Mediterranean trade, was at its height of wealth and power. Literary expression emerged only after the ordeals of conquest, occupation, and Reconstruction, and a nostalgic backward look marks the writing. This was accompanied by a self-conscious awareness of the cultural and racial mix that made New Orleans unique in the United States. The Spanish and

Preface

French cultural presences had mingled with the American frontier thrust and the legacy of Negro slavery to produce something exotic. As a result, the ethnic amalgamation and the accompanying racial tension stimulated George Washington Cable's criticism and Grace King's defense. Those conditions plus an overlay of history developed an atmosphere that drew Lafcadio Hearn's observant eye and held a languorous magnetism for Kate Chopin. In the twentieth century the persistence of the old traditions amid decline and fall has provoked the sensibilities of William Faulkner, Walker Percy, Tennessee Williams, and John Kennedy Toole. A visitor wandering through the streets of the city can still respond to what touched them.

I have subtitled this book "Essays and Meditations" because most of the essayists have fallen under the spell of the New Orleans atmosphere and written in a ruminative, speculative way about the authors whom they are considering. Six of the essays were read at the session "Literary New Orleans" presented at the meeting of the Modern Language Association in New Orleans in December, 1988. The essay on Lafcadio Hearn was prepared for another session at the same scholarly meeting; the essay on Tennessee Williams was written especially for this volume.

Lewis Simpson and I are both grateful to Charles East for help in selecting several of the photographs used as illustrations. I am also grateful to Nadia Kravchenko for help in preparing the typescript of the book.

Temple University   RICHARD S. KENNEDY

LITERARY NEW ORLEANS

George Washington Cable
Courtesy of the Library of Congress

Native Outsider: George Washington Cable

ALICE HALL PETRY

Recently Fairleigh Dickinson University Press published my book on the story collection *Old Creole Days* (1879), by the Louisiana author George Washington Cable (1844–1925). My study is called *A Genius in His Way*, the title coming from one of the many appreciative—indeed, laudatory—reviews that Cable's work garnered, primarily from northern and European reviewers, in his lifetime.[1] The phrase can serve as a reminder that Cable was then regarded as one of the most able creators of short fiction in the world, though he has since fallen to the ranks of secondary authors in American literary scholarship. What is particularly ironic, however, is that readers today have to be re-

---

1. In a review, Charles DeKay said that Cable "is no mere talented writer; he is a genius in his way" (*Scribner's Monthly Magazine*, XVIII [July, 1879], 473).

minded of something else: Cable's race. Surprisingly often, people ask me why I decided to write a book about a black man, and it is difficult not to wonder how Cable, every inch a white Anglo-Saxon Protestant, would feel about being mistaken for one of the people whose plight he depicted with such poignancy, with such startling and daring compassion, in works like *The Grandissimes* (1880). At the same time, it is difficult not to imagine that most of the white residents of nineteenth-century New Orleans, and in particular the Creoles, would find it just that this man who, at least in their eyes, had betrayed New Orleans by insinuating to alien readers that its residents were degenerate, that Creoles, true to the etymology of their name, had the dreaded "taint of Negro blood," and that theirs was a town of violence, gunrunning, and circuses in which beasts battled with only slightly less beastly New Orleanians, could be mistaken for a black himself. When Grace King slammed George Cable on the grounds that he had "stabbed the city in the back . . . in a dastardly way to please the Northern press,"[2] she was, of course, articulating her community's feeling that its raw underbelly, rather more than its charm, was being exposed to the scrutiny of those whose own very different northern and European experiences made them unable to comprehend the southern viewpoint, let alone sympathize with it. It is interesting, in retrospect, that King and her colleagues felt that way, for the evidence appears to suggest that Cable's nonsouthern readers—at least the very early ones—responded quite differently to his writings. In 1923, Robert Underwood Johnson recalled in his book *Remembered Yesterdays* how it was a "fresh and gentle southwest wind that blew into the office" of *Scribner's Monthly Magazine* in 1873 when the manuscript of Cable's story "'Sieur George" arrived there.[3] As the assistant editor at *Scribner's*, Johnson was in an ideal position to appraise the reaction of Richard Watson Gilder and company to the little story by the accountant from New Orleans, and so one can only stand amazed that men who were that astute would equate "'Sieur George" with freshness and gentleness in

2. Quoted by Louis D. Rubin, Jr., in *George W. Cable: The Life and Times of a Southern Heretic* (New York, 1969), 263.
3. Robert Underwood Johnson, *Remembered Yesterdays* (Boston, 1923), 122.

'*Sieur George's*, by Joseph Pennell. Frontispiece in 1883 edition of *Old Creole Days*, Part II.

any form. As dark as anything out of the darkest Conrad, it is a grim and ultimately horrifying story of violence, of would-be incest, and of the eventual reversion to primitivism of a once-proud northern soldier in the enervating Louisiana climate. Rottenness is the story's prevailing quality, with the morally blasted *américain* the rottenest feature on the New Orleans cityscape. The same peculiar twist of critical judgment that led the *Scribner's* staff to respond to the story as if it were a pretty postcard caused King and her cohorts unwittingly to draw national attention to the darker, uglier aspects of Cable's writings by chastising him publicly for betraying his hometown. The telltale vehemence with which the French-language newspaper *L'Abeille* attacked Cable suggests not only that he struck a nerve but that he struck the one his neighbors most wished to conceal. It was just a matter of time before the rest of the world would recognize not only the exotic beauty and originality of his stories but also their complexity—and ultimately their moral rightness, ugly or not.

Of course, Cable was not really from New Orleans. To be sure, he

ALICE HALL PETRY

was born there, but birth is so . . . biological. In spirit, the nineteenth-century argument went, he was an outsider. His mother, Rebecca Boardman, after all, wasn't from New Orleans; worse, she wasn't even from the South. She was an Indianian, no less, whose family was of New England Puritan stock: not one of ours. And that surname, Cable. It is German, surprisingly enough, an Anglicized corruption of Kobell;[4] and though hundreds of Germans settled in Louisiana in the nineteenth century, they were still foreigners, without even a good Acadian—Cajun—name to legitimate them. Cable was clearly a foreigner, an outsider. That was his problem, they said. And in a way King and her allies were right, thank heaven: Cable was just enough of an outsider to be able to see New Orleans objectively—or at least with more objectivity than the average city resident.

Cable seems to have found his own status as a non-native but native-born New Orleanian intriguing, and he probed aspects of it in his fiction, especially—not surprisingly—in his earliest fiction. In the very early tale "'Tite Poulette," for example, the protagonist Kristian Koppig is a well-meaning German clerk who attempts to fathom the complexities of the racial caste system in the South, and the confusing sexual standards it engendered, by observing New Orleans from the most limited point of view possible—a single, tiny window overlooking one little-used street. As a writer who owed much to the example of Nathaniel Hawthorne, whose semiconcealed observers often cannot fully grasp the complexities of what they are watching, Cable seems to have appreciated thoroughly that no outsider—and perhaps especially not someone from a climate as cold and a gene pool as pure as Germany's—could begin to grasp the nuances of New Orleans in the nineteenth century, where such sensitivity to the matter of race prevailed that although 'Tite Poulette is herself black by Louisiana legal standards, she would not be recognized as such even in blond-haired, blue-eyed Germany. Like Kristian Koppig himself, Cable had the best Christian impulses in studying and writing about New Orleans, but as the surname Koppig—that is, "headstrong"—suggests, no one knew better than he that he was stubbornly trying to grasp, convey, and

4. Arlin Turner, *George W. Cable: A Biography* (Baton Rouge, 1966), 4n2.

4

challenge a society truly too complex for a first-generation New Orleanian to fathom.

All this is not to say, however, that Cable approached his subject matter with a cold eye and a sneer. Perhaps too much has been made of his Puritan background, his marriage to the rather straitlaced Louise Bartlett, and his dismissal from the staff of the *Picayune* in 1871, allegedly for declining to review a play—the theater, of course, being a shameless waste of time and spirit. Cable himself was quick to point out that refusing to go to a play was hardly grounds for dismissal and that the incident really was the coup de grace for a journalistic career most charitably described as well intended. Indeed, there is ample evidence that Cable had always enjoyed reading plays, even those of the scandalous Molière, and that eventually he began not only to attend the theater but to love it. In brief, whatever his upbringing and his alleged puritanical temperament, he seems to have harbored a fondness for the dramatic, the sensual—yes, the forbidden. What better place to indulge it than in New Orleans, the exotic milieu that gave the world jambalaya, Cayetano's Circus, and quadroon balls? If Cable did indeed have a streak of puritanism in him, it was sorely put to the test in that tempting environment; and perhaps it was the resulting struggle in him that is responsible for the power of a story like "'Sieur George." When, at the end of the tale, 'Sieur George has lost his home and career, has gambled away a fortune entrusted to him by playing the notoriously corrupt lottery, and has alienated the young girl he raised as his own child by suggesting they elope, his only possible course is to repair to "the prairies" surrounding the Crescent City, where he sleeps in the open air, like the animal he has become. One can well imagine that his is the fate, spun out to melodramatic extremes, that could have befallen another George, Cable himself, had he simply written stories extolling the superficial charms of the Creole world, ignored the harsh realities underlying the exotic surface of that society, pandered to the popular tastes of his northern readers—and thrived financially in the process. Instead he chose a more challenging course, resisted the attractions of Creole life, risked the alienation of his neighbors in his increasingly vocal pleas for civil rights, and often endured financial hardships rather than compromise his vision.

5

Café des Exilés, by Joseph Pennell. Frontispiece in 1883 edition of *Old Creole Days*, Part I.

That meant leaving New Orleans. After a series of visits to the North, Cable settled briefly in tony Simsbury, Connecticut, in 1884, and then moved to somewhat less tony Northampton, Massachusetts, the following year. Northampton was to be the center of his existence for the last forty years of his life. It was probably the most personally agreeable move he could have made: he was closer to his fellow lecturer and "twin of genius," Mark Twain, the most notorious resident of Hartford, Connecticut; he had easier access to Broadway, one of the loves of his life; and he was in contact with northern intellectuals, with a public and a press that were receptive to his liberal views regarding social reform in the South, in particular civil rights. But artistically the move to Northampton was not to his advantage. Unlike the many writers who must live in Paris or Havana or Rome in order to write about their American hometowns, Cable seems, ironically enough, to have needed to be in the closest possible contact with his subjects in order to write about them artistically. Perhaps, indeed, he was already so much an outsider in New Orleans that to live in Massachusetts made him doubly one—sequestered from New Orleans' allures and surrounded by appreciative northern critics, to be sure, but so out of touch with his material that he became oddly dry and preachy. Such qualities are just barely detectable in his earliest writings, most of which are essentially thinly veiled allegories redolent of Hawthorne

6

and anticipatory of Flannery O'Connor. But the streak of pedantry did not become rampant until physical distance kept the genuine allures of New Orleans from continuing as ballast or leavening for his most scathing criticisms of racism, of prison conditions, of the arbitrary cruelties of the Code Noir, and of the incapacity of either society or what he termed the "cobwebby Church" to challenge the injustices he perceived. *Dr. Sevier* and *John March, Southerner* and *The Cavalier* are important social documents, but not particularly artistic ones.

None of this, however, seems to have bothered Cable. As he became an undisguised social critic with public statements such as "The Freedman's Case in Equity" (1885) and *The Negro Question* (1890), he clearly came also to see artistry as far less important than human rights. And is that so wrong?

So how would this sensual puritan, this non-native native-born New Orleanian feel about being mistaken for a black in 1992? I think he would see it as a tribute to his achievements, to his capacity to identify so thoroughly with the subjects of his heartfelt concern that he became, in effect, one of them. I think George Washington Cable would open a bottle of Jax beer and give his books a little toast.

Grace King
Courtesy of John M. Coxe

The Patrician Voice: Grace King

ROBERT BUSH

No writer has been more intimately connected with the city of New Orleans than Grace King. Her patrician family background, the impact of the Civil War on her emotional growth, her drive to write fiction and history about the city—all of these elements produced the ideal cultural and creative citizen, who at the end of her life in 1932 had long since achieved a dominant position in the intellectual life of the city.

The ambition that led to the writing of thirteen books, of which eleven are concerned with New Orleans, began with the Civil War experience of her family during her years between the ages of ten and fourteen. She was ten when Admiral Farragut sailed up the Mississippi and occupied the city with Federal troops for the duration of the war and the Reconstruction period. King was a deeply sensitive child who from her bedroom window watched the flames along the levee as the Confederates burned cotton and other goods to prevent their coming into the hands of the enemy.[1] The word *enemy* entered her vocabulary, and she was thereafter inclined to regard the North with a degree of suspicion. If she had been older at the time, the events of the war might not have left so lasting a trauma on her consciousness.

The Kings escaped through enemy lines to take refuge on their sugar plantation in mosquito-infested southern Louisiana. When they returned to New Orleans in 1865, their town house had been appropriated and their sole asset was the father's law practice, which cost him years to revive. He settled his family in the eastern limits of the city, where the rents for modest workmen's houses were cheap. The Kings' situation was hardly desperate, but they suffered the humiliation of living in poverty after they had been prominent residents of the city.[2]

Although King was reared a Presbyterian, she attended French schools, where she mixed easily with girls from Creole families, who were of course Catholic. Culturally she developed a bias for French culture and civilization. The strongest early influence in that direction was the historian Charles Gayarré, who in her youth represented the Franco-Spanish past of the city. When she and one of her sisters visited the Gayarrés at their plantation on the Mississippi-Louisiana border, she learned what conversation was, and the French paintings and furniture of the country home reinforced her preference for French civilization.[3] As Gayarré grew older and King launched her career with the story "Monsieur Motte" and the biography of Bienville, it seemed that she had become Gayarré's successor as the champion of the city's individuality in fiction and in history.

---

1. Grace King, *Memories of a Southern Woman of Letters* (New York, 1932), 4–5.
2. Robert Bush, *Grace King: A Southern Destiny* (Baton Rouge, 1983), 16–19.
3. *Ibid.*, 26–27.

King's writing career to a large extent sprang from her loyalty to the city of New Orleans and especially to the Creoles. Her characteristic emotion was the old Roman attitude of *pietas*—a devotion to family, city, and country. For her, *country* meant the South or the fallen Confederacy. The young George Washington Cable, eight years her senior, was able to comprehend the South with greater objectivity. His standard of truth was Emersonian in its self-reliance. His first novel, *The Grandissimes* (1880), characterized the early-nineteenth-century Creoles as brutal and insensitive slave owners whose historical origins were rarely aristocratic. Gayarré entered into a literary fray with Cable over this, and the young King agreed with the point of view of her mentor and other representatives of New Orleans' establishment.

When the ambitious Cotton Centennial Exposition opened in 1884, Grace King's writing career had not yet begun. Her father had died in 1881, but her three brothers had established their careers and the family had progressed from working-class Delery Street to respectable North Rampart Street. They had overcome the economic disadvantages of Reconstruction and could again hold their heads up in New Orleans society. During this period in the 1880s the King family established their reputation as representative New Orleanians who accepted important visitors to the city with warm hospitality. At their home a northerner could learn the point of view of the postwar establishment and enjoy himself at the same time. Among the visitors during the exposition were Julia Ward Howe and Richard Watson Gilder.

The exposition was still open in the spring of 1885, when Gilder visited the city and met King at a dinner given by Mrs. Howe. The editor of *Scribner's Monthly Magazine* (later *Century Magazine*) was surprised to find himself on the defensive on the question of Cable. Gilder was proud of having discovered Cable and having published his early stories, later collected in *Old Creole Days* (1879). After the supper, King found herself paired off with Gilder as the party walked home, and in their conversation Gilder asked her "about the inimical stand taken by the People of New Orleans against George Cable and his works." Her answer, recalled late in life, was,

10

The Patrician Voice: Grace King

I hastened to enlighten him to the effect that Cable proclaimed his preference for colored people over white and assumed the inevitable superiority—according to his theories—of the quadroons over the creoles. He was a native of New Orleans and had been well treated by its people, and yet he stabbed the city in the back, as we felt, in a dastardly way to please the Northern press.

. . . He listened to me with icy indifference, and the rest of our walk was accomplished in silence except for one remark. "Why," he said, "if Cable is so false to you, why do not some of you write better?"[4]

King took the challenge altogether seriously, and as she saw bias in Cable's interpretation of race relations in New Orleans, she hoped to set the record straight. Her first story, "Monsieur Motte," with its three sequels, became her first volume of fiction, fortunately sponsored by Charles Dudley Warner, one of the northern friends her family had entertained. The obvious question about the volume is to what extent it is an answer of the establishment to Cable, the apostate. There is no direct answer since King was never a propagandist. She was herself in the tradition of Cable in that she used the gold mine of materials she found in the characteristic local life of New Orleans. But where Cable's early fiction had exploited romantically the city's antebellum experience, King's *Monsieur Motte* dealt with New Orleans in her own time—Reconstruction and after. She maintained that she was a realist and that in depicting such an unstandardized locale as the city she was treating romantic material realistically.[5]

"Monsieur Motte" is the story of Marcélite, a quadroon hairdresser who is the former slave of a patrician Creole family. She is so devoted to her former owners, now dead, that she labors out of affection for their orphaned schoolgirl daughter, paying for her education in a private school. Marcélite is aware that for a black to support an impoverished young lady would cause embarrassment or disgrace to her; to avoid doing the girl harm she pretends that the support

4. King, *Memories*, 59–60.
5. See Grace King to Fred Lewis Pattee, January 19, 1915, in *Grace King of New Orleans: A Selection of Her Writings*, ed. Robert Bush (Baton Rouge, 1973), 398.

comes from Monsieur Motte, an invented uncle. Insofar as the story is an answer to Cable, King implied that within the city of New Orleans black servants, especially women, were often so well treated by their masters that their devotion carried on to Reconstruction times in acts of love and sacrifice. King was to affirm that she had herself observed the good treatment white masters gave and the devotion former slaves returned. In those early years of her career she wrote Warner that "the only vocation I feel is the desire to show you that a Southerner and a white person is not ashamed to acknowledge a dependence on negroes, nor to proclaim the love that exists between the two races, a love which in the end will destroy all differences in color; or rather I had better say—that that love is the only thing which can do it."[6]

By the mid-1890s, King had sufficiently exploited her theme of race relations to write what few southern women have written: history. Her *New Orleans: The Place and the People* (1895) is a very readable example of American municipal history, ordinarily a pedestrian kind of writing. But King had fully researched her subject and recognized in it character and drama of a kind found in few other cities' histories. Her models were the nineteenth-century literary historians Francis Parkman and John Fiske, whom she admired. Praised by William Dean Howells and Edmund Wilson, the book contributed to a national awareness of the uniqueness of New Orleans.

In 1916, King published an episodic novel, *The Pleasant Ways of St. Médard*, based on the King family's experience following the war, when they lived on Delery Street. No book so poignantly depicts the life of impoverished southern patricians in the topsy-turvy world of Reconstruction. The loyal Confederate family suffers in poverty while the ignorant San Antonios have risen to wealth through their collaboration with the occupation forces. The more famous authors of Reconstruction novels usually chose to interpret the period in terms of violence and sentimental romance. King avoided both those approaches and portrayed the everyday life of families and their neighbors during

6. Grace King to Charles Dudley Warner, November 22, 1885, in Bush's *Grace King: A Southern Destiny,* 61.

1749 Coliseum Street, King's home from 1904 to 1932
Photograph by David Coxe, courtesy of John M. Coxe

a period marked by suffering that was relieved only by the hope that the time would come when fate and personal energy would restore the dispossessed to their prewar position.

During the first third of the twentieth century King and her sisters continued as leaders in the cultural development of their city. King held open house on Friday afternoons, when she welcomed friends for conversation and tea at her permanent home at 1749 Coliseum Street. In Paris in 1891 and 1892 she had been welcomed into women's salons; in New Orleans she created a variation of the Paris salon. At her teas she certainly stimulated the conversation but probably did not dominate it as her French friends had done.

King's interests in politics and in the progress of women were strong but always second to her literary preoccupations. She was politically conservative, a Democrat in the old southern sense. But in her writings, especially in her fiction, she showed a special sympathy for women, whose cause she championed over what she considered the dominance of the southern male. In that she was unusually progres-

13

ROBERT BUSH

sive. Part of the motivation for her career was her drive to achieve financial independence from her three working brothers. Once she succeeded in that, she descended from the traditional pedestal on which southern ladies were placed and became the working woman active in behalf of other working women. She played a supporting role in feminist organizations, but she insisted that she was never a propagandist. Influenced by Isabella Beecher Hooker and Julia Ward Howe, she was an early advocate of women's suffrage. In 1888, she gained the attention of Susan B. Anthony, who invited her to speak on the suffrage question at a convention in Washington, but she did not accept. In 1917, King founded the Southern Women's Economic and Political Association to sponsor studies of the economic life and history of the South. But her greatest local accomplishment was her labor for the Louisiana Historical Society.

Gayarré and King were among a small group who revived the Louisiana Historical Society in 1893. She served as secretary for many years and as editor of *Publications of the Louisiana Historical Society* from 1895 to 1917. At the turn of the century she had urged the city to use the Cabildo, on Jackson Square, as a historical museum. In 1909, her idea was made a reality when the Cabildo became a center for the society.[7]

In her youth, King was an attractive woman with serious suitors, but she did not marry. She was perhaps too learned to be the southern lady that the typical Louisiana male found interesting. Like the father in *The Pleasant Ways of St. Médard,* the conventional male had a "perfect horror of learned ladies, 'blue stockings' who quote Latin and Greek and talk algebra and astronomy. He likes charming ladies, those who are good looking, who dress well, have exquisite manners, who talk well, who have tact."[8]

King was one of a number of southern women of her generation who helped change the stereotype of the southern lady, who maintained the old style and grace but combined them with learning and

7. For a full account of the public activities of Grace King, see Etta Reid Lyles, "A Transitional Generation: Grace King's World, 1852–1932" (Ph.D. dissertation, University of Maryland, 1987), 222–77.
8. Grace King, *The Pleasant Ways of St. Médard* (New York, 1916), 48.

14

thinking. The city of New Orleans was in a sense a surrogate for a husband. She was the Protestant American brought up in admiration of the Franco-Spanish culture. Entranced by the city's romance, she made it the enterprise of her career. As historian, novelist, and social intellectual, she contributed as much to the improvement of the city's culture as anyone of her time.

Lafcadio Hearn. From *Lafcadio Hearn: Life and Letters*, by Elizabeth Bisland (1906).

Cultural Translator: Lafcadio Hearn

HEPHZIBAH ROSKELLY

For the nearly twenty years he spent in the United States, Lafcadio
Hearn remained an outsider. An orphan of an English father and a
Greek mother, he had fled a harsh convent school in England and arrived in Cincinnati in 1869, frightened, miserable, and without resources. His oddly small figure and neurotically shy demeanor—one
of his Cincinnati editors was later to call him the "distorted brownie"—
kept him from prospering there, and he was close to starving when he
was taken in by a printer, Henry Ward Watkin. Watkin taught him the
journalist's trade, got him a job as a writer, and several years later
helped him make his way to New Orleans, where he lived until he emi-

grated to the Orient. The printer who helped him was my great-grand-mother's cousin, and I first learned about Hearn because of her. Family and geographical connections fed her lifelong interest in Hearn. In 1931, P. D. Perkins was producing a bibliography of Hearn's work, and Mère, who had lived in New Orleans most of her life, aided him by reviewing all the data she had accumulated on the writer over the years—clippings mostly—and recording all the places he had lived in New Orleans. Riding down to the Quarter on the streetcar, she photo-graphed many of those spots and sent the information along to Per-kins. Her adventure became a tale in our house, and Lafcadio Hearn be-came a household word. It was his New Orleans life and the New Orleans stories we knew about, and only when I was grown did I dis-cover that Hearn had accomplished something besides them.

The rest of the world knows about Hearn because of his Japanese stories. As one of the first outsiders to live in that part of the world, he translated a whole culture to Western readers. He was an honorary citizen, an adopted son, and a respected university professor at the University of Tokyo and later at Kyoto, and he became immersed in Japanese custom and tradition. At the same time, he remained outside it by virtue of his heritage and his translator's mind, and his dual role of participant and spectator made his observation rich and accurate. Though critics generally recognize the Japanese writing as Hearn's best, he had learned the art of cultural translation long before his sojourn in Japan. In New Orleans, he went about the task of translating for the majority culture the cultures of the other populations of the city at the fringe of a newly progressive South: the Creole, the Cajun, the black. Just as he was to do in Japan ten years later, he immersed himself in the customs of the cultures he observed. In the old part of the city, the Quarter, he used the paradox of being at once participant and ob-server to explore the tensions apparent to him, oppositions between Old and New South and between dark and light residents. In explor-ing the tensions and oppositions, he became both a local colorist and ethnographer of the cultures that lived on the margin, and at the heart, of the city.

When Hearn arrived in New Orleans in 1877, he saw immediately the paradoxes and tensions. He had escaped the unfriendly northern climate of Cincinnati on a riverboat headed south, just as ten years before that he had escaped the even unfriendlier climate of his orphanage school in England, dreaming of warmth and security. New Orleans offered the hope of both, of some financial stability, and of a measure of literary fame for him as a journalist in a locale that seemed to him almost supernaturally lovely. But a month after he arrived he wrote to Watkin, "The wealth of the world is here—unworked gold in the ore. . . . The paradise of the South is here, deserted and half in ruins. I never beheld anything so beautiful and so sad. When I saw it first—sunrise over Louisiana—the tears sprang to my eyes. It was like young death—a dead bride crowned with orange flowers—a dead face that asked for a kiss. I cannot say how fair and rich and beautiful this dead South is. It has fascinated me."[1] This passage shows how quickly Hearn recognized the contradictions and used them in his writing. For if New Orleans was beautiful, it was also dangerous, continually beset by plagues of yellow fever and breakbone fever and malaria, and if it held promise, it also held its promise at bay. Ten years beyond the Civil War, the city remained devastated by the conflict's effects and still suffered under a venal Reconstruction government. As Lyle Saxon writes in his travel book *Fabulous New Orleans,* "The period of Reconstruction in Louisiana is the most tragic part of its story. New Orleans had been one of the richest—if not the richest—city in the country. It became one of the poorest. Not only were men stripped of all they had, but the basis of their commercial life had been destroyed."[2] Like the city, Hearn struggled for survival, sometimes eating only every other day at the nickel plate-lunch restaurants in the Quarter, changing his residence often when he could no longer pay his landladies, suffering from an attack of dengue (breakbone fever) that affected his already poor vision. He had been in the city nearly a year before he found work at the New Orleans *Item,* and by then he had lost some of his

1. Elizabeth Bisland, *Lafcadio Hearn: Life and Letters* (2 vols.; Boston, 1906), I, 42–43.
2. Lyle Saxon, *Fabulous New Orleans* (New York, 1928), 255.

18

exhilaration. Still, the city continued to captivate him. "It is better to live here in sackcloth and ashes," he wrote during his first year, "than to own the whole State of Ohio."[3]

For the next ten years, Hearn wrote essays, editorials, sketches, and features that explored the cultures of the city, particularly those that lived on the other side of Canal Street, the side opposite what he, like the Creole, was to call the *américain*. The New South represented by the *américain* seemed to those who lived in the Vieux Carré to be commercial, humorless, and passionless, and they opposed such qualities both overtly and unconsciously. Hearn, who had already decided the Western Anglo-Saxon way was not his, gravitated to the other cultures in part because of the personal peculiarities that kept him an outsider in the majority community. A childhood accident had left him sightless in one eye, and his good eye was "milky and rolling," as Henry Watkin described it: he could read only with the book held a few inches from his face. The odd stare he assumed, as well as his stature and extreme shyness, made him a curious object in the newsroom and on the bustling streets of the city. Hearn had discovered that in untraditional settings his differences were tolerated or ignored. In Cincinnati he had made his home on the levee with black riverboaters and had even provoked a small furor in the community by living with a young black woman there. It seemed natural for him to choose to live on the Creole side of Canal Street and to record his fascination with cultures apart from the mainstream.

Hearn has been labeled a local colorist, because he used picturesque detail and dialect to authenticate the culture he described. But his impulse in the tales was not primarily nostalgic but ethnographic. Hearn used language to achieve what the educational anthropologist Frederick Erickson argues is the primary objective of the ethnographer: to make the strange familiar and the familiar strange to the larger culture. "Upon entering a non-Western society the fieldworker doesn't have to make the familiar strange because everything is unfamiliar and much is strange," Erickson says. "But when describing

3. Bisland, *Lafcadio Hearn*, I, 215.

HEPHZIBAH ROSKELLY

institutions of his or her own society, the ethnographer must adopt the critical stance of the philosopher, continually questioning the grounds of the conventional, examining the obvious, that is so taken for granted by cultural insiders that it becomes invisible to them."⁴ Placed in the camp of neither the outsiders nor the insiders of the cultures he observed, Hearn saw the unusual in everyday events on the Creole side of the city. New Orleans readers of the *Item* and the *Times-Democrat* did not find the sights of street vendors, laundresses, or even potion peddlers unfamiliar. But through Hearn's eyes, the majority group became aware of the strangeness and beauty in familiar sights: gypsies singing on the levee at night, children reciting charms to ward off the evil eye, white chalk marks on pillars to signal a death from fever.

Hearn's eye was unsentimental, and his ear was sensitive. He was vitally interested in language; in fact during his time in New Orleans, he published essays on the Creole patois in *Harper's*, wrote *Gombo Zhebes: A Dictionary of Creole Proverbs* and a Creole cookbook, and compiled a collection of gypsy songs. The intense study of language makes his use of local dialect in the New Orleans stories both clear and organic. "Voices of Dawn," one of his early vignettes for the *Item*, brings the streets of New Orleans alive by mimicking the competing voices and varying dialects of the street vendors who crowded beneath his window each morning to push their stock. Using spelling and word order to let the reader hear the accents of black, Italian, French, and Cajun, Hearn cataloged the hawker who called, "Chick-EN, Madamma," the sellers of "Lemons, Ap-Pulls, Straw-BARE-eries," the Italian who offered "Lagniappe-y," and the black man who chanted, "Cantel-lop-ah Fresha and fine, Jus from the vine, Only a dime."⁵

Hearn used local dialect often in his New Orleans stories. Like the local colorist, he often provided dialectal spelling, though, unlike the local colorist, seldom at the expense of readability. In Hearn's stories, the dialectal spelling and frequent Italian or Cajun phrases helped him in describing the culture more intensely, as though he lived it, and one

4. Frederick Erickson, "What Makes School Ethnography Ethnographic?" *Anthropology and Education Quarterly*, XV (1984), 62.
5. Lafcadio Hearn, "Voices of Dawn," in *Creole Sketches* (Boston, 1924), 197.

20

Hearn's sketch accompanying "Morning Calls—Very Early," New Orleans *Item*, July 7, 1880

way he created the illusion of being an insider in the culture was to duplicate dialect. Moreover, the dialectal signals in essays like "Voices of Dawn" are clues to the nonverbal character of the culture: its liveliness, its humor. Hearn's punctuation gives similar indications. In "Ghosteses," a tale about a boarder who imagines ghosts and keeps his fellow apartment dwellers awake at nights, Hearn used the run-on sentence, the dash, and the quick paragraph break to mimic the speech of the owner of the pension who tells the story: "So he become afraid more to bed go, and ven he mount he not himself sleep, but valk all night on de gallery, one lantern in his hand, and shoes all vat be of mos' heavy for drive away ghosteses—tata—tatatatata—all de long of de night." The boarders cure him by constructing a "fantome," and he falls down the stairs. "Never again he not speak and soon he be dead, and no person much sorry himself." [6] To complete the cycle, the boarder becomes a real ghost haunting the apartment house. The language of the apartment owner in the story demonstrates his personality and

6. Hearn, "Ghosteses," in *Creole Sketches*, 37.

typifies it, but the dialect also provides insights into what Hearn took to be values of the Creole character: relationships with others, respect for the dead, communal responsibility.

Hearn found value in the very differences of the cultures he wrote about, and his writing about them became a translation of sorts, exposing the life of the "other" New Orleans to Gilded Age New Orleans. His attempts at translating alternate culture for dominant culture involved him in interpretation, in revealing the essence of what he saw. Hearn was an accomplished translator, producing masterly translations of Zola, Gautier, and Baudelaire while he was in New Orleans—and by the time he emigrated to Japan, a detailed philosophical position on the role of the translator. Speaking of his translations, he wrote in a letter to a friend, "I want to interpret the body and soul of the original and of the society which produced it." [7]

All his work is in this sense translation, suggests Beongcheon Yu in a critical study of Hearn's work. It reflects a desire to transmit the value and the values of the culture as well as to produce both a faithful and an artistic rendering of texts. The danger in the kind of interpretation Hearn attempted is what Yu regards as an occasional "unwarranted subjectivism." [8] Hearn himself seemed aware that his advocacy of the cultures he described might be taken as unwarranted. His technique for masking his advocacy was to vary his narrative technique by making the narrator not always an insider who knows and speaks the dialect but sometimes an outsider who aligns himself with his majority readers by almost apologetically removing himself from the scene he has been unfolding. In "Voices of Dawn," for example, Hearn concluded, "If any one has a little leisure and a little turn for amusement, he can certainly have plenty of fun while listening to the voices of the peddlers entering his room together with the first liquid gold of sunrise." [9] In "Creole Servant Girls," an admiring description of the underlife of the black and Creole servants who were viewed as family retainers by their Anglo-Saxon employers, Hearn climaxed his pointed

7. Bisland, *Lafcadio Hearn*, I, 112.
8. Beongcheon Yu, *An Ape of Gods: The Art and Thought of Lafcadio Hearn* (Detroit, 1964), 18–19.
9. Hearn, "Voices of Dawn," 201.

critique by asserting that "they do not like American or English speaking people," but he then lamely concluded the vignette by shrugging off his political statement: "The type is fast disappearing, but it certainly affords one of the most extraordinary studies of human nature possible to conceive." [10]

Hearn's last words often ring false in the sketches, and a more successful technique is his creation of another kind of narrator, an outsider who is not so much majority commentator as naïve foil for the wiser native. In "Why Crabs Are Boiled Alive," a Cajun conducts a one-sided conversation with a foolish outsider who has come to taste the local cuisine. Taunting the visitor's too tender sensibilities, the Cajun asks, "And for why you not have of crab? Because one must dem boil live?" In this sketch, only a paragraph long, Hearn reveals the tension between majority and minority culture as the Cajun explains impatiently why crabs must be boiled live. He concludes, "You not can dem bleed until dey die, for dat dey not have blood. You not can stick to dem troo de brain, for dat dey be same like you—dey not have of brain." [11]

One of Hearn's most interesting stories is "Creole Character," where the narrator appears to take on the values of the majority culture while subtly demonstrating the superior qualities of the alternate one. The story recounts the construction of an awning in the Quarter. The first few sentences seem clearly ethnocentric: "It was not a difficult job to put up a wooden awning about the corner grocery—two stout Irishmen would have done it in an hour." The gulf between Creole idleness and American industry is made explicit throughout the story. The Creole carpenters will abandon their assigned task at any provocation—a lovely woman who crosses the street, a slight rain, a mad dog they feel compelled to chase—and they talk to everybody in the neighborhood who passes by. Finally, they set to work, hammering in time to a Creole tune they sing. The narrator finishes the story by noting sternly that "that awning still remains in a wild and savage condition of incompleteness." The narrative appears at first derogatory, and

10. Hearn, "Creole Servant Girls," in *Creole Sketches*, 163.
11. Hearn, "Why Crabs Are Boiled Alive," in *Creole Sketches*, 59.

Hearn's sketch accompanying "Ultra-Canal," New Orleans *Item,* July 17, 1880

the narrator condescending, as he implies that the Creole is like his awning, "wild and savage." But near the end of the story the narrator admiringly quotes the workmen who sing, "Ce nes pas bapteme, travail comme ça," and he ends with a wistful, "Life was too short." Relating what he exposes as a joyful story, the narrator shows the reader that he too thinks life is too short to be concerned only with awnings.[12]

The dual-voiced narrator, majority observer and minority advocate, is a device Hearn used often in his most successful stories. One of his friends and benefactors in New Orleans, Dr. George Gould, wrote, "His was almost a unique expertness of entering into the spirit of his models, re-feeling their emotions, reimagining their thought and art, and reclothing it with the often somewhat hard and stiff material of English weaving."[13] Using that technique, Hearn was able to call into question the American work ethic, which seemed so opposed to life in the Quarter. The opening line to "A Tale of a Fan," one of Hearn's stories in the *Fantastics,* laughs at the industry of the *américain:* "Bah!

12. Hearn, "The Creole Character," in *Creole Sketches,* 82–84.
13. George Gould, *Concerning Lafcadio Hearn* (Philadelphia, 1908), 69–70.

24

It is too hot to write anything about anything practical and serious—let us dream dreams."[14] Another tale in the same collection, "Les Coulisses," is even more contemptuous of those who condemn dreamers: "The spell is broken for a moment by Beings garbed in the everyday attire of the nineteenth-century, who have devoted themselves to the work of destruction and reconstruction—to whom dreamers are an abomination and idlers behind the scene a vexation of spirit."[15] In these tales, Hearn puts himself squarely underneath the Creole awning.

Hearn's subjectivity is obvious to any reader of these stories. But it may not be "unwarranted" as an attempt at translation. Erickson points out that it is essential for an ethnographer to understand how personal viewpoints affect description. "It was I who was there doing the field work," Erickson says, "not somebody else. My fundamental assumptions and prejudices are part of me. The ethnographer cannot separate herself from the object being described. The method is not that of objectivity, but of disciplined subjectivity."[16] Hearn was careful to be disciplined as he attempted to avoid what he saw as a failing of local-color writing, the one-sided sentimentality that pervaded its descriptions. "The art itself must be founded on catholic principles—upon those touches of nature which make the whole world kin," he wrote in a piece about local-color writing for *Harper's*. "It must be independent of the nativity or nationality of the artist."[17] To Hearn, the artist has the large responsibility of finding a catholic standpoint from which to depict the culture. "Literature is never intended to expound schemes of philosophy and wise drawn theories concerning the organic structure of the social fabric," he says in "Science and Literature," adding, "It is better that philosophy and fiction should be kept apart."[18]

If Hearn was sincere in his critique of local-color writing, his attempt was to make not a philosophical or political statement about the cultures in New Orleans but an artistic one. Nevertheless, his politi-

14. Hearn, "A Tale of a Fan," in *Fantastics and Other Fancies* (Boston, 1914), 78.
15. Hearn, "Les Coulisses," in *Fantastics and Other Fancies*, 84.
16. Erickson, "What Makes School Ethnography Ethnographic?" 62.
17. Hearn, "Local Color Writing," in *Selected Writings* (New York, 1949), 68.
18. Hearn, "Science and Literature," in *Selected Writings*, 23.

cal statement is clear in the stories. And in editorials and a few of the sketches, Hearn lobbied unashamedly for the alternate life he witnessed in the Quarter. "A Creole Courtyard" begins, "Without, roared the Iron Age, the angry waves of American traffic; within, one heard only the murmur of the languid fountain; . . . without, it was the year 1879; within, it was the epoch of the Spanish domination." So clearly attractive is the other life, so superior to the angry waves on the American side, that the narrator concludes sarcastically, "And yet some people wonder that some other people never care to cross Canal Street."[19] Hearn validated the cultures on the fringe whose alternate ways of knowing he called southern or Latin, ways that valued the natural, the holistic, the mystical, and the unexplained. He worked hard to show the contribution of the variant cultures to the life of the city.

But his artistic statement is clear as well. He played with the effects of juxtaposition, the untraditional and the strange shouldered against the normal workaday world. Of course, the most symbolic New Orleans gesture toward exposing paradoxes is Mardi Gras, and Hearn wrote glowingly about it in his sketch "Dawn of Carnival":

> The night cometh in which we take no note of time, and forget that we are living in a practical age which mostly relegates romance to printed pages and merriment to the state: and the glorious night is approaching—this quaint old-time night, star-jeweled, fantastically robed; and the blue river is bearing us fleets of white boats thronged with strangers who doubtless are dreaming of lights and music, the tepid, perfumed air of Rex's Palace, . . . who will dance the dance of the Carnival until blue day puts out at once the trembling tapers of the stars and lights of the great ball.[20]

Embedded in Carnival is the philosophical tension between American and Creole, including the paradoxes that fascinated Hearn in New Orleans, paradoxes that countless writers and filmmakers since him have explored, arising from the conflicting pulls of progress and tradition, beauty and decadence, youth and death, reality and fantasy. These are the odd pairs he saw in the life of the city. And the culture of the Yankee, which valued business and daylight and no nonsense, was

19. Hearn, "A Creole Courtyard," in *Creole Sketches*, 81.
20. Hearn, "The Dawn of the Carnival," in *Creole Sketches*, 90–92.

Hearn leaving New York for Japan. Sketch by C. D. Weldon, from *Lafcadio Hearn's American Days*, by Edward L. Tinker (1924).

held at bay symbolically by Canal Street, the strip one crossed to enter an older world where pleasure and darkness and mystery overcame the practical. Hearn's studies of the life of alternate cultures helped him locate metaphors for an essential tension he was finally to identify as a polarity between Eastern and Western ways of knowing. After ten years Hearn left the paradoxes of New Orleans to encounter Eastern thought in even more dramatic ways. But his work in New Orleans taught him how to draw the fine line marking off cultural boundaries and the artistic expression of them. The New Orleans stories belong in the literature of a city that Hearn realized was not the dead bride he had written to Watkin about in his first days there but a living beauty,

vital and rich because there were two sides to Canal Street. I like thinking of my great-grandmother on the streetcar, crossing Canal into the
Quarter to help document the record of Hearn's time in the city. He
would have liked that, an acknowledgment of the other side of Canal
Street as well as a recognition of his part in preserving it.

Kate Chopin
By permission of the Missouri Historical Society, Negative No. POR-C-25

New Orleans as Metaphor: Kate Chopin

ANNE ROWE

"I always feel so sorry for women who don't like to walk; they miss so much—so many rare little glimpses of life; and we women learn so little of life on the whole." [1]

These are the words spoken by Edna Pontellier to her admirer, Robert LeBrun, in Kate Chopin's novel *The Awakening*. Edna has earlier said that, of late, "I have got into the habit of expressing myself" (336). Both statements could have just as easily been made by Chopin herself, for they could refer to her acquired habit of expressing herself even if it appeared "unwomanly," and also her habit, exercised often in New Orleans, of walking about alone, gaining rare little glimpses of life.

Chopin's experience in New Orleans was exceptionally beneficial to

---

1. Kate Chopin, *The Awakening and Selected Stories* (New York, 1981), 337. Hereafter page numbers will be cited parenthetically in the text.

her as a writer. The city offered her an array of scenes and a variety of experiences that influenced her in her formative years as a writer. Later, and most often when she no longer lived in New Orleans, she recalled those scenes and recast her impressions into some of her best fiction.

Since most readers are not familiar with the sequence of events in Chopin's life, it is important to underscore the extent of her exposure to New Orleans. Kate O'Flaherty was born in 1851 in St. Louis, Missouri, and attended the St. Louis Academy of the Sacred Heart, graduating in 1868. She made her first visit to New Orleans in April, 1869, and she recorded her impressions in her journal: "N. Orleans I liked immensely; it is so clean—so white and green. Although in April, we had profusions of flowers—strawberries and even black berries." [2]

Her first impressions of New Orleans prefigure her continuing admiration for the city. During the visit, she met a well-known singer and was inspired by that woman's success. And on a lesser note, it is reported that on this visit the eighteen-year-old girl smoked her first cigarette. Then, as now, New Orleans offered all sorts of excitement.

Chopin's next and more prolonged association with New Orleans came little more than a year later. In June, 1870, she married Oscar Chopin of a French Creole family from Natchitoches Parish, in the northwestern part of Louisiana. After a three-month honeymoon journey abroad, the couple settled in New Orleans, where they lived until Oscar Chopin's cotton brokerage failed in 1879 and they moved to his family's estate on the Cane River near Natchitoches.

One has to be amazed that in the eight or so years that Chopin lived in New Orleans she learned and absorbed as much as she did. Not only were there frequent visits back to St. Louis and summers at the coastal resort of Grand Isle, about ninety miles from New Orleans, but she also gave birth to six children—five sons and a daughter—during that time. On second thought, maybe it is understandable that she enjoyed getting out of the house as often as possible. At any rate, her comments in her diary show that she enjoyed walking unaccompanied around the city or riding the mule-drawn streetcars, "observing the

2. Cited by Barbara C. Ewell in *Kate Chopin* (New York, 1986), 10.

A house on Prytania Street in the Garden District in the late 1930s
Courtesy of the State Library of Louisiana

cosmopolitan bustle of the French Market of Canal Street or the waterfront, where her husband's . . . business originated." It has also been noted that although her diary entries on New Orleans were "not deliberately literary," they give evidence that she was absorbing a wealth of detail she could use later in her fiction.[3]

After the family moved from New Orleans in 1879, Chopin never lived there again. Oscar Chopin died of malaria three years later, and she returned to St. Louis in 1884, where she made her home until her death in 1904. Although her physical ties with New Orleans and Louisiana became limited to visits, the last of which took place in 1900, her literary association was far from over. Chopin's memory of New Orleans and of Natchitoches Parish served as the basis for much of her writing, beginning with the local-color short stories she published from 1889 on and culminating with the novel *The Awakening* in 1889. And just as her fiction became more developed, more polished, so did her use of the New Orleans settings become more complex and artfully rendered.

3. *Ibid.*, 14.

It has often been said that Chopin is a writer who transcended the local-color mode. She achieved her first popularity by publishing stories in the genre, so popular in the 1880s and 1890s, which by emphasizing uniqueness of place, quaint characters, and contrived plots, suited a large national audience. With the publication of *The Awakening*, she moved beyond local color, in the opinion of many critics. Yet her use of setting, in this case her treatment of New Orleans, is one of the strongest and clearest reasons that her work has not been forgotten. Although some of her short stories are placed in New Orleans, her fullest treatment and use of the New Orleans setting is in *The Awakening*. The early negative reaction to the novel, which is about a young woman who, awakening to life, finds that her role as wife and mother is not fulfilling her needs and desires, is well documented. My concern here, though, is to show how well Chopin used New Orleans not only to give color and texture to her novel but also to develop characterization and plot within the novel metaphorically.

Although the first part of *The Awakening* is set on Grand Isle, where Edna and Leonce Pontellier and other Creole families are vacationing, New Orleans continually intrudes. The life-style at Grand Isle, relaxed and informal, is juxtaposed against a busier, more structured life in the city. Leonce, for example, joins his family only on weekends, in order to pursue his business in New Orleans, but even when he is at Grand Isle he reads the New Orleans papers—and is disappointed when the news is a day old. Leonce is in the habit of going off to Klein's hotel, where the New Orleans men congregate, preferring their company to that of the women and children.

Chopin writes of Edna that "that summer at Grand Isle she began to loosen a little the mantle of reserve that has always enveloped her" (190). Edna, in her seven years of marriage, has followed a conventional, orderly life. This summer, however, she begins to change, and a part of the change comes from receiving the attention of a young Creole, Robert LeBrun, who, like Leonce, works in New Orleans but is less absorbed by the world of business.

Robert, who every summer "devotes" himself to a woman at Grand Isle, but in a Platonic sense only, eventually falls in love with Edna, and it is significant, I think, that he determines to pursue his fortunes in

New Orleans as Metaphor: Kate Chopin

The French Opera House, destroyed by fire in 1919
Courtesy of the Louisiana State Museum

Mexico once he realizes that he and Edna may be going beyond the bounds of his usual summer courtship. Chopin's use of New Orleans is important when Edna says to Robert, "Why I was planning to be together, thinking how pleasant it would be to see you in the city next winter." "So was I," he blurted. "Perhaps that's the—" (240). Robert's sentence is left unfinished, but what he implies is that what is acceptable at Grand Isle would take on a serious aspect were they to see each other in New Orleans. The city, then, in the opening section of the book is ever present, serving always as a foil to Grand Isle, as a place where ritual, social distinctions, and material success are acknowledged and important.

As the story shifts to New Orleans, the city becomes even more important. No longer is New Orleans simply a counterpoint to Grand Isle; it takes on primary importance. It has been remarked that one of the most striking uses of setting by Chopin is in the description of the homes of the major women in the novel—Edna Pontellier and the two characters who serve as foils to her, Adele Ratignolle, the "mother-woman," content, even blissful, in her role as wife and mother (with a new baby arriving every eighteen months or so), and Mademoiselle

Reisz, the unpleasant, unattractive spinster who is portrayed as the true artist in the novel, a gifted pianist devoted to her music.[4]

Even though Chopin describes the homes of these women largely through interior scenes, a method highly characteristic, perhaps, of women writers, the exterior locale, New Orleans, is an important feature of the setting. The Pontellier house is described as

> a very charming home on Esplanade Street in New Orleans. It was a large, double cottage, with a broad front veranda, whose round, fluted columns supported the sloping roof. The house was painted a dazzling white; the outside shutters, or jalousies, were green. In the yard, which was kept scrupulously neat, were flowers and plants of every description which flourished in South Louisiana. Within doors the appointments were perfect after the conventional type. The softest carpets and rugs covered the floors; rich and tasteful tapestries hung at doors and windows. There were paintings, selected with judgement and discrimination, upon the walls. The cut glass, the silver, the heavy damask which daily appeared upon the table were the envy of many women whose husbands were less generous than Mr. Pontellier. (247)

Chopin accomplishes many things in this paragraph, including demonstrating Leonce's concern with show and his conventional taste. The fact that Edna is, in some ways, simply another of his elegant possessions emerges here as well. But also appearing are the unique qualities of the New Orleans double cottage, the lush plant life, and the "white and green" that the writer noted in her diary on her first trip to New Orleans. Within the house all is conventional and orderly; without, there are possibilities for renewal and growth, and Edna will soon discover them.

In contrast to Edna's traditional, well-appointed home is Adele Ratignolle's abode:

> The Ratignolles lived at no great distance from Edna's home, on the corner of a side street, where Monsieur Ratignolle owned and conducted a drug store which enjoyed a steady and prosperous trade. . . . His family lived in commodious apartments over the store, having an entrance on the side

4. Robert White, "Inner and Outer Space in *The Awakening,*" *Mosaic,* XVII (1984), 97–109.

within the porte cochiere. There was something which Edna thought very French, very foreign about their whole manner of living. (225)

Edna is beginning to be attracted by her friend's exemption from the need to keep up with New Orleans society in the way Leonce wishes her to do. She is also intrigued by what she perceives as a European way of living over one's shop, a life-style that attests to the cosmopolitan qualities of New Orleans. But there are other aspects of Adele's life that are less attractive to Edna, including Adele's utter devotion to housekeeping. When Edna arrives for a visit, Adele is sorting the laundry even though she has a servant who might attend to that task. Adele ushers Edna into her "salon, where it was cool and sweet with the odor of great roses that stood upon the hearth in jars" (256). It is significant that in this description there is no presentation of exterior scenes. Flowers, domesticated ones at that, are cut and brought inside to live for a while. The flowers and their beauty are counterparts to Adele herself, who when the family is in New Orleans seldom goes outdoors. Not for her are the perambulations around the city so characteristic of Edna.

In great contrast to the houses of both Edna and Adele is the apartment of Mademoiselle Reisz, the pianist:

> There were plenty of windows in her little front room. They were for the most part dingy, but as they were nearly always open it did not make so much difference. They often admitted into the room a good deal of smoke and soot; but at the same time all the light and air that there was came through them. From her windows could be seen the crescent of the river, the masts of ships and the big chimneys of the Mississippi steamers. A magnificent piano crowded the apartment. (266)

We learn several things here. Mademoiselle Reisz is no housekeeper: she does not clean her windows. Her art is central to her life: the piano crowds her apartment. That is the way it should be, for Chopin offers Mademoiselle Reisz as one who sacrifices all other aspects of her life for her work. It is also important, however, that although the pianist is crowded in a small apartment, her windows are almost always open, allowing the outside sights and sounds to enter. And the sight that is present is one of New Orleans' most striking: the crescent of the river, with the masts of the ships. Mademoiselle Reisz has her windows open to New Orleans and, by way of the Mississippi, to the world.[5]

Also evocative of mood is a scene in a New Orleans suburb where Edna has one of her last meetings with Robert LeBrun:

> There was a garden out in the suburbs, a small, leafy corner, with a few green tables under the orange trees. An old cat slept all day on the stone step in the sun, and an old *mulatresse* slept her idle hours away in her chair at the open window, till some one happened to knock on one of the green tables. She had milk and cream cheese to sell, and bread and butter. There was no one who could make such excellent coffee or fry a chicken to golden brown as she.
>
> The place was too modest to attract the attention of people of fashion, and so quiet as to have escaped the notice of those in search of pleasure and dissipation. (334)

In this description Chopin shows the reader that Edna is not merely a pleasure-seeker and that, unlike Leonce, she is not a person of fashion. She discovers the garden while out on one of her walks, and the discovery is one of the rewards won by those who are willing to seek out and explore. It is significant too that Chopin emphasizes the gardenlike, almost Edenic quality of this setting—peaceful, restful, in contrast to the bustle of the city.[6] Just as Edna has been emerging from her passive, almost cocoonlike self, here the indoor, domesticated settings of earlier in the novel are brought out of doors. Here one can eat and read in a setting of flowers, of greenery and light. The homey comforts of Adele's house, the outside lights that come in only through the open windows of Mademoiselle Reisz's apartment, the reading materials found in Edna's home—all seem brought together in the little garden scene in the suburbs.

The Awakening does not end on such an idyllic note, of course, but the garden scene seems like a paradisiacal respite before the conclusion of the novel. The setting seems the culmination of the variety of New Orleans scenes Chopin created vividly and with great detail.

As Edna Pontellier's knowledge of New Orleans grows beyond her

5. *Ibid.,* 104.
6. *Ibid.,* 106.

home and her fixed daily routine, so does her knowledge of herself. Her growth exhibits Chopin's ability to create a rich, complex character. As Chopin's writing transcended the local-color mode, her use of setting became not only backdrop but metaphor. New Orleans became an integral part of the story. It was for her a rich source of material, material she fashioned with intricate detail and great artistry.

William Faulkner
By permission of the Louise Meadow Collection

The Brooding Air of the Past: William Faulkner

W. KENNETH HOLDITCH

In two centuries the old French Quarter of New Orleans has under-gone incredible changes. From a small walled village, it grew to one of the wealthiest cities in North America, glistening brightly among American capitals during its golden age, then enduring federal occupa-tion through the years of the Civil War and Reconstruction. By the start of the twentieth century it was well into a serious decline, which has never been truly reversed. By the 1920s the wealthy and powerful French and Spanish residents had been replaced by poor Italian labor-ers and merchants and their families. The Old French Opera House, social and cultural center of the district, had been destroyed by fire in 1919, and the once-affluent Vieux Carré had become for the most part a slum, shunned by the *américains* uptown who had once been made unwelcome there by the Creoles.

The Brooding Air of the Past: William Faulkner

Perhaps only an imagination as powerful as that of William Faulkner's could re-create for us what that haunted area must have been like in its twilight age, but the period photographs by Arnold Genthe, E. J. Bellocq, and Pops Whitesell reveal rows of three-story carriage houses interspersed with brick-between-post Creole cottages, early-nineteenth-century Greek Revival houses, and the Victorianized structures of a later period, as well as historical landmarks, all in varying states of disrepair—beautiful ghosts still enshrouded by that aura Faulkner called the "atmosphere of a bygone and more gracious age." Yet, even in decay, how much more elegant and romantic they seem than some of the garish Disneyland renovations of today, in which architects supposedly endeavoring to preserve have often instead effaced. It was to the Quarter of those photographers that Faulkner came in November, 1924—an appropriate gathering place for artists and writers, this once grand old city faded into a slum, this "courtesan, not old and yet no longer young," as he wrote of her, "who shuns the sunlight that the illusion of her former glory be preserved." [1]

In the 1970s, acting on the suggestion of Carvel Collins, I interviewed all I could locate of those who had been part of the Quarter's artistic colony in the 1920s and had been caricatured in *Sherwood Anderson and Other Famous Creoles,* a collection of drawings by William Spratling, with the text by Faulkner. In addition, I interviewed Albert Goldstein, who with several others had founded *The Double Dealer,* and George Healy, longtime editor of the *Times-Picayune.* Insofar as my inquiries of the surviving "famous Creoles" relate to Faulkner, it seems that most of them can be summarized under three basic questions: What was Faulkner like? What did he do? What did he say? A hasty evaluation of the responses I received might lead a cynic to assume that Faulkner did nothing but drink and write, that he said nothing but rather sat in stony silence, listening, and depending on which "famous Creole" one believes, that he was either a delightful and trustworthy friend and companion or a vain and arrogant man who forgot his old friends when he became famous.

Why did they come, these writers and artists from town and city,

1. William Faulkner, *New Orleans Sketches* (New York, 1968), 13.

from Midwest, East, and South? The answer lies partly in the literary mystique of the city, that blend of myth and reality which has from the beginning marked authors' atittudes toward New Orleans. Sherwood Anderson, an ardent exponent of the mystique, found New Orleans the perfect blend of the two best ethnic cultures in the world, French and black, and published an open invitation urging writers to come to the "most civilized place I've found in America."[2] Another reason for the Quarter's becoming a Greenwich Village South during the most interesting literary period in the city's history surely involved its reputation as the Big Easy, the City That Care Forgot. Storyville had been closed by the Department of the Navy in 1917, but prostitution, though limited and less blatant, still flourished, and the prevalent political corruption—a hallmark of the city, past and present—made vice not only easily available but gave it the appearance of, if not respectability, at least acceptability and appeal.

Prohibition seems hardly to have fazed the city that A. J. Leibling, Walker Percy, and others have likened to a banana republic with much more kinship to the Mediterranean and the Caribbean than to the rest of the United States. For the artists and writers the availability of liquor, albeit of questionable quality, seems to have been a consideration of some importance, surely one of significance for Faulkner, who arrived bringing his own supply of corn whiskey, allegedly made on his family plantation, "just in case." Sherwood Anderson's wife reports in her autobiography, *Miss Elizabeth,* that there were at the time several speakeasies in the Pontalba apartments on Jackson Square, but one wonders why they should have existed, considering that there were Quarter bars that never ceased to operate and that almost any of the large number of Italian groceries sold alcohol openly. Papa Joe Joseph, for example, dispensed whatever was available from his store on the corner of Royal and St. Peter streets. Marc Antony mentioned that Papa Joe sat in a chair in front of his business in good weather and that upstairs tenants of surrounding buildings yelled down to him before lowering a basket with money and receiving a bottle in exchange. "Alcohol was the catalyst that held us together," Keith Temple said, and Genevieve Pitot stated that they all drank, perhaps because of rather

2. H. M. Jones, ed., *Letters of Sherwood Anderson* (Boston, 1953), 87.

Faulkner's first apartment, in Pirate's Alley
  By permission of Craig Dietz

than in spite of Prohibition (that "terrible, terrible dictation sort of thing: You can't have liquor!") or perhaps because "everyone of us in those days had a sense of life, of joyousness; we were all looking forward to something, and we celebrated that."[3]

3. Marc Antony, conversations with author, November 1, 1974; Keith Temple, conversation with author, January 11, 1975; Genevieve Pitot, conversation with author, November 20, 1974.

For a Francophile such as Faulkner, convinced that one never escapes the past, the Quarter, then as now essentially a self-contained village, was glamorous and appealing. Never a joiner, he was only peripherally a part of the ragtag collection of artists who lived and worked there, but he made friends—Sherwood Anderson, Roark Bradford, John Dos Passos, Oliver Lafarge, William Spratling, and others—who were integral influences on the fiction he was to produce. The passage in *Absalom, Absalom!* in which Mr. Compson imagines Henry Sutpen in pre–Civil War New Orleans perhaps parallels Faulkner's own first response—and that of many a Mississippi youth through the decades—to a place so different from the small town of his past:

> I can imagine him, with his puritan heritage—that heritage peculiarly Anglo-Saxon—of fierce proud mysticism and that ability to be ashamed of ignorance and inexperience, in that city foreign and paradoxical with its atmosphere at once fatal and languorous, at once feminine and steel-hard—this grim humorless yokel out of a granite heritage where even the houses, let alone clothing and conduct, are built in the image of a jealous and sadistic Jehovah, put suddenly down in a place whose denizens had created their All-Powerful and His supporting hierarchy-chorus of beautiful saints and handsome angels in the image of their houses and personal ornaments and voluptuous lives . . . a place created for and by voluptuousness, the abashless and unabashed senses.[4]

Faulkner presents Latin Catholic New Orleans here, be it noted, in contrast not to the rest of the nation but only to the Protestant South. It was a world at odds with what he had known, and he soaked it up as he had soaked up all the sense impressions and experiences of his youth and early manhood. He drank coffee at the Morning Call, a century-old stand in the French Market, ate at restaurants that in those days were usually cheap, always good: Galatoire's, Arnaud's, Broussard's, Madame Petrie's, Madame Gaye's, Victor's, Turci's (opened on Decatur Street by two opera singers, husband and wife, who were stranded in the city when their company folded). He went to parties, where he watched and listened, and he accompanied Sherwood Anderson on visits to local characters such as Aunt Rose Arnold, retired pro-

4. William Faulkner, *Absalom, Absalom!* (New York, 1936), 108–109.

prietor of a house of prostitution who stood over six feet tall, favored an attire in the style of Lillian Russell with muttonchop sleeves, corsets, and stays, and entertained the writers with stories of her occupation. Living in close proximity to the old Place d'Armes, now known as Jackson Square—at the Andersons' apartment in the Pontalba and in the two apartments he shared with Spratling, the first in 1925 on Orleans Alley (now renamed Pirate's Alley to attract the tourist trade), the second in 1926 on Cabildo Alley—Faulkner could observe the, to him, foreign doings of local Latin Catholics at the cathedral. Corpus Christi Day celebrations, for example, were still major events in the 1920s in New Orleans, with parades of Italian children, all dressed in white, moving through the streets to the square. As Carvel Collins has pointed out, Corpus Christi Day, which fell on June 2 in 1910, serves a special symbolic function in the structure of *The Sound and the Fury*—only one example of how Faulkner stored up and used experiences.

During his months in New Orleans in 1925 and 1926, Faulkner underwent an astounding transformation, some credit for which must be given to the city in which it occurred. When he arrived, he was in essence a fairly competent poet too much under the influence of the heady decadent romanticism of the late Victorians, and when he returned to Oxford, Mississippi, to live, he had published one novel, finished a second, and established the coordinates for Yoknapatawpha County and envisioned much of the great fiction he would locate in his "little postage stamp of native soil."[5] In addition, during that fertile period in New Orleans he produced the *Mirrors of Chartres Street* and *New Orleans Sketches* for the major newspaper of the city, the *Times-Picayune*, and for the *Double Dealer* respectively. When one considers the influence of this place and that time upon the emerging writer, the remarks of the "famous Creoles" and their contemporaries upon their friend and associate who went on to achieve a fame far surpassing any they could envision for him take on considerable significance.

George Healy, who knew Faulkner at Ole Miss at the time the aspiring author was fired from the post office, met him again in New

5. George Plimpton, ed., *Writers at Work: The Paris Review Interviews* (New York, 1958), 141.

The Morning Call, a coffeehouse in the French Market
Courtesy of the State Library of Louisiana

Orleans. Healy, who was then a reporter on the *Times-Picayune*, the newspaper of which he would later be editor, recalled that Faulkner "used to drop by the office two or three nights a week." Healy described vividly the almost nightly parties in the Quarter, with everyone "drinking bathtub gin and if they could latch onto it any grain alcohol. I remember an artists' ball given once a year by the Arts and Crafts Club to raise money, a costume ball. Keith Temple went as the bishop of Little Woods, and Bill Harvey went as the bishop of Bucktown, which of course were two New Orleans places of questionable fame." On their way to the party, the two "mendicant friars" collected several dollars in the streets. Wearing street clothes rather than a costume, Healy was "one of the few people in the party that wasn't either half naked or dressed like a bishop. I remember Bill was having a big time that night, observing. He used to love to stand in the corner and oversee. He was a people watcher. And I'd drop over and chat to him—he wasn't in costume either—and he would pass observations about one of the participants or another." [6] Healy recalled Phil Stone, Faulkner's

6. George Healy, conversation with author, October 16, 1974.

44

mentor from Oxford, Mississippi, stating that when the young writer was in the French Quarter he lived on only five dollars a week.

Keith Temple in the 1920s shared an apartment, nicknamed the Wigwam, with Oliver LaFarge, the anthropologist and authority on southwest Indians who later wrote several novels, including the Pulitzer Prize–winning *Laughing Boy*. Temple, a longtime political cartoonist on local newspapers, spoke disparagingly of Faulkner as a man who "kept to himself, walked the streets by himself, did not even look healthy."[7] Although there is evidence that he and Faulkner were rather close friends and at one point made a trip to New York together, Temple in the 1970s could recall only the "unhappy poor drunk" he had seen asleep on the bricks of patios after overindulgence.

One of the most exciting aspects of literary life in New Orleans in the 1920s was the publication of a remarkable literary journal, the *Double Dealer,* established in 1921 as an answer to H. L. Mencken's calling the South the "Sahara of the Bozart." An amazing magazine that continued to appear until 1926 and achieved national reputation and renown, the *Double Dealer* published Faulkner's early *New Orleans Sketches* as well as work by Anderson, Hemingway, and Hart Crane. One founder of the journal, Albert Goldstein, recalled the young Faulkner as moody and withdrawn. His strongest memory, however, was of the later Faulkner, who returned in 1950 to accept the French Legion of Honor. The two men arrived for the ceremony ahead of everyone else and Goldstein introduced himself to the author: "I said, 'I didn't know you in those days, but all of the people that you knew were friends of mine'—and, of course, I always knew that he was a very shy person, almost introverted—and I remember that everything I said he would answer with, 'Well, yes, yes.' 'Of course you remember Lyle Saxon and Roark Bradford,' and he said, 'Yes, yes.' No elaboration. Then . . . the ceremony took place and I never saw him again, but I have such a vivid recollection of that short conversation in which the only word he uttered was *yes*."[8]

Harold Levy, another founder of the *Double Dealer* and the mu-

7. Marc Antony, conversation with author, November 1, 1974.
8. Albert Goldstein, conversation with author, October 21, 1974.

sical director of Le Petit Theatre, had been a classmate of John Dos Passos' at Harvard and was a good friend of Sherwood Anderson's. Levy's apartment in the Pontalba building on St. Ann Street was a gathering place for artists, musicians, and writers. Some of them who worked in the Quarter got together there at noon every weekday, and as they ate lunch and drank wine, one of them read from a copy of James Joyce's *Ulysses,* banned from the United States at that time, which a member of the group had smuggled into the country. Levy recalled Faulkner's stopping by one evening, probably with Spratling, and remarking in the course of the visit that he was having difficulty completing a poem on which he had been working. Levy examined it and supplied him with a line. Later, when the poem was finished, Faulkner gave Levy a holograph copy bearing the inscription "To Harold Levy who helped me write this when my muse failed."[9] "The Faun," published in the *Double Dealer* in April, 1925, contains the inscription "To H. L." Levy's last encounter with Faulkner was, he believed, at the time of Roark Bradford's funeral in 1948, when the two met by chance on Bourbon Street and exchanged a few words.

Marc Antony was a close friend of Sherwood Anderson's for several decades. Antony and his wife, Lucille, entertained in their Quarter apartment Thomas Wolfe, Gertrude Stein, Carl Sandburg, and other authors of the twenties and thirties. Lucille was a partner with Anderson's wife, Elizabeth, in an interior decorating business and dress shop in the Antonys' building on the corner of St. Peter Street and Cabildo Alley. It was into the attic apartment of the Antonys' house that Faulkner and Spratling moved after their return from Europe in 1926; here they produced *Sherwood Anderson and Other Famous Creoles,* published in December of that year. In Antony's recollections, Faulkner comes alive as complex and intriguing, a man who had a "curious way of sort of appearing and disappearing":

> Well, he was a strange character, to my way of thinking. He sort of made you feel like sometimes he was slinking around. Wore old tweed clothes that always seemed to belong to somebody else; they always looked like they were bigger than for Faulkner. And the general impression was he al-

9. Harold Levy, conversation with author, November 23, 1974.

46

ways had a newspaper package under his arm, which could have been a bottle of whiskey. I don't recall his wearing a hat. And he was friendly, but at times he seemed withdrawn.[10]

With a certain bitterness, Antony remembered that after Faulkner became famous he had no time for his old friends. Once, hearing that he was in town, Antony left a message for him at the hotel, but Faulkner never called. "And then walking by one day, he was coming out of the hotel and he deliberately ignored me, walked right by me. And he did that with practically every friend of his in New Orleans, and these were the days when he was well dressed, wore beautiful clothes, and wore a hat."[11] Antony would perhaps have been less offended had he known that the novelist's mother reported that when her son was engrossed in an idea, he sometimes passed even her by without so much as a nod.

Antony's memory of Faulkner is studded with gems in the form of stories about the man: Faulkner, just back from working on a shrimp lugger, leaving the St. Regis Restaurant, on Royal Street, barefoot, then returning to retrieve his shoes; Faulkner, Marc and Lucille, Spratling, Lyle Saxon, Sherwood Anderson, and other "Creoles" on a one-day yacht cruise on Lake Pontchartrain, where they were besieged by mosquitoes; Faulkner with his advance for *Mosquitoes,* his second novel, holding a dinner at Galatoire's for the unsuspecting people he had satirized in the novel. Some of them never forgave the insult of his portrayal, Antony recalled; Lillian Marcus, for example, "hated the way Bill described her in the book," even though she claimed that she had never read it.[12]

A guidebook to New Orleans says that Faulkner made his living there leading tours. That odd and inaccurate bit of information has its origin in his unsatisfactory one-day stint in such a role. For the Chamber of Commerce, Antony and his wife operated a guide service to introduce out-of-towners attending conventions to the Quarter. They relied on whatever local friends were available as guides, and on one

10. Marc Antony, conversation with author, November 1, 1974.
11. *Ibid.*
12. *Ibid.*

occasion they "got hold of Bill Faulkner," Antony recalled. "Well, there must have been eight or nine of us, each with a group, and the groups spaced about half a block apart, you know, but before the thing was over practically everybody was following Bill, because . . . we would walk down one block and we would say, 'Now this is the Haunted House,' and we'd tell the story about the Haunted House and we would walk another block or two before we would find something else to talk about, but whenever anybody would say, 'Well, this is an interesting house. What happened there?' Bill would go ahead and spiel something, so he was telling stories everywhere and he had everybody in the whole convention practically following him with his built-up stories."[13]

My favorite account of Faulkner in New Orleans is that of Genevieve Pitot, perhaps because she was an especially exciting and interesting survivor of the group. A great-great-granddaughter of the first elected mayor of New Orleans, Pitot, as she preferred to be called, studied music as a young woman with Alfred Cortot, the great pianist, in Paris, then returned to New Orleans to the excitement of the 1920s. Later she moved to New York, where she became friends with such famous contemporaries as George Gershwin, Aaron Copland, Agnes De Mille, and Buckminster Fuller, and wrote the ballet scores for more than twenty Broadway musicals, including *Kiss Me Kate* and *Li'l Abner*. Perhaps the only authentic Creole among the group, she described herself fifty years after the fact as a flapper, "wild and woolly and a crazy musician," who went to one of the Beaux Arts balls costumed as Salome and did the dance of the seven veils, much to the chagrin of some of her relatives who read about it in the *Times-Picayune*. Pitot had nothing but praise for Faulkner, a "very warm" man, a "great humanitarian," with "great insight into people." Between them, she recalled, there was a rapport, and he was "an enabler to me. I know he liked me. He never talked to me very much, but he liked my spirit and the youthfulness of me and the drive that I had. There was no doubt that he was attracted and interested in my vitality." Like several from the period, she recalled that at parties he "sat on the floor or

13. *Ibid.*

on a chair in the corner . . . and he was never without a drink. I guess there might have been a bottle next to him. People would go and talk to him. But I never recall Faulkner milling around with people and going from one to another. He sat in a corner, watching people, studying people; I think he was doing that for his literature, the things he wanted to write." Looking at the drawing of Cabildo Alley in *Sherwood Anderson and Other Famous Creoles* that depicts the attic where Faulkner and Spratling created the work, Pitot laughed, "Oh, I remember going up those stairs to that apartment, way on the top. It's still there; you can't see it. . . . It's right under the roof; the windows are about that big. How they lived in those days under that hot roof in this heat and no air conditioning, I don't know." [14] It was from this fourth-floor apartment that the two creators of *Sherwood Anderson and Other Famous Creoles* in a belated burst of youthful mischief sometimes took aim with BBs at passersby in Cabildo Alley below. From this apartment one night, the two of them, annoyed by the constant presence of Sherwood Anderson's teenage son Robert, stripped the young man, painted his penis blue, and pushed him out into the alleyway, locking the door behind him.

Faulkner was to return to New Orleans on several occasions during the years, most notably in 1934 for the opening of Shushan Airport, a visit that inspired the creation of *Pylon,* in which a central character, the reporter, was based on the New Orleans newspaperman Hermann Deutsch. In 1951, he was back in the city, accompanied that time by his wife, Estelle, to receive the French Legion of Honor award, an honor in which he professed to take more pride than in the Nobel Prize.

At the end of the thirties, another young aspiring writer from Mississippi, Tennessee Williams, came to New Orleans. He was later to say of the city that he found in it a freedom he had never before known, and the shock of it against the basic puritanism of his character gave him material about which he continued to write for the rest of his career. Much the same might be said about Faulkner, who fifteen years before the playwright became a resident of the French Quarter, had experienced the culture shock with like results.

14. Genevieve Pitot, conversation with author, November 20, 1974.

What exactly did Faulkner derive from his months in New Orleans? That freedom of which Williams spoke was surely one of the benefits for the young writer in the 1920s, but there were other influences and advantages perhaps of more significance. Despite his eventually turning against Sherwood Anderson—in the age-old story of the pupil who outstrips the master—the advice and support of the older writer, then in the prime of his fame, was surely of importance. In addition, Faulkner fell deeply in love in the city with a young woman named Helen Baird. It was, from the start apparently, a doomed relationship but one the influence of which he never quite escaped; indeed, perhaps he never wanted to be rid of the memory of the woman to whom he dedicated *Mosquitoes* and for whom he created two "private volumes" of poetry, for she continued to turn up in various guises in his work, from Patricia Robyn, of *Mosquitoes,* to Linda Snopes, of *The Mansion.* Most of all, however, surely one of the most significant benefits of the author's stay in New Orleans was the rich, brooding air of the past that hangs over the city even now and that in the 1920s was much more intense and pervading. The *New Orleans Sketches* and other passages from his work—most saliently the passage from *Absalom, Absalom!* about the imagined first response of Henry Sutpen to the city—indicate the degree to which this atmosphere, redolent of the past, of mystery and romance, intrigued and inspired one of the greatest American novelists.

Mr. and Mrs. Walker Percy as Binx and Kate in *The Moviegoer*
Courtesy of Mrs. Walker Percy

Pilgrim in the City: Walker Percy

LEWIS LAWSON

I cannot say exactly when Walker Percy made his first visit to New Orleans, though I imagine that it was as a teenager living with his Uncle Will up in Greenville, Mississippi. He certainly was there in his late twenties, in 1946, expressly to court Mary Bernice Townsend, a nurse he had known for at least six years. They were married on November 7, 1946, in a local Baptist church. The newlyweds spent their first months in Uncle Will's summer home, near Sewanee, Tennessee, but one Tennessee winter was enough to convince them that they wanted to live in New Orleans. So they returned in 1947, living first at the Pontchartrain Hotel, while they looked for a house to rent. Robert Coles describes the rental property they found on Calhoun Street as a "nice old house at the edge of [the] Garden District."[1] Here Percy

---

1. Robert Coles, *Walker Percy: An American Search* (Boston, 1978), 71.

LEWIS LAWSON

worked on "The Charterhouse" and "The Gramercy Winner," both unpublished novels, and on the first draft of The Moviegoer. He remained a tenant until 1950, when he drove across Lake Pontchartrain and decided at once to live in Covington, a pleasant nonplace. In "Why I Live Where I Live," he gives a possible reason for his move: "The occupational hazard of the writer in New Orleans is a variety of the French flu, which might also be called the Vieux Carré syndrome. One is apt to turn fey, potter about a patio, and write feuilletons and vignettes or catty romans à clef, a pleasant enough life but for me too seductive."[2] In other words, as he put it on another occasion, "A sense of place can decay to the merely bizarre."[3]

Once in Covington, though, Percy turned to look back at New Orleans, in his essay "New Orleans Mon Amour."[4] Most readers, both those who have read his novels and those who have only read about them, are probably somewhat surprised at the temperateness of the piece. A characteristic balance is struck in the first paragraph: "If the American city does not go to hell in the next few years, it will not be the likes of Dallas or Grosse Point which will work its deliverance, or Berkeley or New Haven, or Santa Fe or La Jolla. But New Orleans might. Just as New Orleans hit upon jazz, the only unique American contribution to art, and hit upon it almost by accident and despite itself, it could also hit upon a way out of the hell which has overtaken the American city."

Here, of course, is the old apocalyptic rumbling that always disturbs the Percy landscape, but here is also that slight possibility, also always present, that humanity might just avoid the fate of Sodom and Gomorrah. Americans, however, should put not their faith in the utopia provided by models of the city of wealth (Dallas or Grosse Point), of the city of intellectualism (Berkeley or New Haven), or of the city of aestheticism (Santa Fe or La Jolla). Each of them is built upon a devo-

2. Walker Percy, "Why I Live Where I Live," Esquire, XCIII (April, 1980), 36.
3. Walker Percy, "Virtues and Vices in the Southern Literary Renascence," Commonweal, May 11, 1962, p. 181.
4. Walker Percy, "New Orleans Mon Amour," Harper's, CCXXXVII (September, 1968), 80–82, 86, 88, 90.

52

tion to a single aspect of human experience and a contempt for all other aspects. Thus incomplete, each is unreal.

Real cities attract all forms of human thought and behavior and always have. Indeed, it seems that it is the very variegatedness of a city that attracts new immigrants. But now it also seems that many American cities have reached a crisis of diversity, in which the center does not hold. Since New Orleans is probably first among the diverse, why has it not exploded? An investigation of this nonevent is the body of Percy's piece.

Percy confesses a guarded optimism for New Orleans, not because of "sociological indices" but because of a "quality of air," a "property of space," and a "certain persisting non-malevolence." The quality of air results from the presence of so many ethnic and racial traditions, a condition conducive to infinite "rotations," to use another Percy term: Laissez bons rotations rouler! The property of space is a subtle merging of private and public domains. Percy cites New York as a city in which the two domains are absolutely separated: a person sheds all humanity who goes outdoors. He offers Mobile as the opposite: a person acts in public as if still in private. New Orleans is that city, probably more a happy medium than an unhappy one, in which people ordinarily mind their own business but don't step over someone needing help. The nonmalevolence results from a mutually moderating effect by the two major behavioral patterns, an Anglo-Saxon seriousness of purpose and a Mediterranean mellowness: the "marriage of George Babbitt and Marianne" is how Percy puts it.

Percy believes that so far the good qualities of both traditions have predominated more often than not but shudders to think what will happen if the bad qualities of the two life-styles get the upper hand. He is not denying the historical reality of slavery as an absolute evil but is simply saying that the condition of the black, though it has never been good, could get even worse. The picture so far presented is free of institutional influence. Thus having pointed out the danger of sheer drift, Percy announces that there must be more activity by individuals working through institutions to maintain and develop the bonds of community. He identifies the business establishment, the communications

A St. Charles Avenue streetcar
By permission of Grant L. Robertson

media, the church, and higher education, applauding their good initiatives and regretting the occasions when they betray lack of nerve or selfishness.

To conclude his essay, he cites Mardi Gras as the case example of both the special promise and the special problems of New Orleans. Mardi Gras is a very desirable institution, for it is a "universal celebration of a public occasion by private, social, and neighborhood groups." What is wrong with it is that while it has opened itself to the George Babbitt desire for commercialization, it has remained closed to full black participation. Implicit in both the increasing commercialization and the continuing segregation is the gradual disappearance of any religious significance. Then Percy sounds his cautionary note by going from the parade route to a much more general thoroughfare: "New Orleans' people—black and white—may yet manage to get on the right road. The city may still detour hell but it will take some doing." Percy thus ends where he began: all hell may break loose if enough humans do not do something. But if enough humans do do something, then all heaven could just as easily break loose. In "Stoicism in the South," he sums up in one sentence his attitude as a Christian toward the city: "The urban plebs is not the mass which is to be abandoned to its own barbaric devices, but the lump to be leavened."[5]

And in an interview he has said exactly what New Orleans means to him, speaking apropos of *The Moviegoer:*

> So many people ask me why I didn't write about the French Quarter in New Orleans instead of Gentilly. Who cares about Gentilly? Gentilly looks like any other place. All the alienated writers say it's anonymous. Well, that's what my main character, Binx Bolling, liked about it. He liked the quality of the sky out there in Gentilly. He liked the parochial school across the street, made of brick and aluminum and glass. He had an appreciation for these mass manufactured objects. It's very easy to sneer at mass society or the American suburb, but there are many beauties there. So, this business of alienation can certainly be overdone. But, of course, alienation, after all, is nothing more or less than a very ancient, orthodox Christian doctrine. Man is alienated by the nature of his being here. He is here as a stranger and as a pilgrim, which is the way alienation is conceived in my books.[6]

Percy's description of man "as a stranger and as a pilgrim" is a direct reference to 1 Peter 2:11. But even more, it is an allusion to Saint Augustine, whose great work, *The City of God,* developed the idea of the pilgrim, the wayfarer, the peregrinator, for Catholic institutional literature. To several interviewers, Percy has confessed Saint Augustine to be a thinker to whom he is especially indebted. It suddenly becomes clear why Percy structured his essay on New Orleans around the theme of a trip, by asserting first that New Orleans was on the road to hell or its alternative and by then particularizing the illustration of that trip in Mardi Gras. In the larger sense, then, when Percy speaks of New Orleans, he is speaking of the entire world writ small, even as Mardi Gras is New Orleans writ small.

In *The City of God,* Saint Augustine brings together the concept of

---

5. Walker Percy, "Stoicism in the South," *Commonweal,* July 6, 1956, p. 344.
6. Carlton Cremeens, "Walker Percy, the Man and the Novelist: An Interview," in *Conversations with Walker Percy,* ed. Lewis A. Lawson and Victor A. Kramer (Jackson, Miss., 1985), 26.

the pilgrim in the actual city and the concept of the alternative cities, the City of God and the Earthly City, or Jerusalem and Babylon, or the homes of Abel and of Cain. The dynamic germ of Christianity, then, is the idea that man, of his own free will, is always on the way to one or other of these cities. Saint Augustine, it should be noted, did not assert that the City of God was the actual church or that the actual city was the Earthly City. He referred, rather, to "mystical cities." He was speaking figuratively, in order to contrast opposing absolute spiritual realities, love of God versus love of self, conversion toward God versus aversion from God. In "New Orleans Mon Amour," Percy is appealing to people who seek the peace that results from loving God and their fellowmen but do not seek a secular peace that must be bought by ignoring evil.

The choice between the two figurative cities is prominent in both of Percy's New Orleans novels, *The Moviegoer* and *Lancelot*. Indeed, in *The Moviegoer* he uses the actuality of Mardi Gras, the world in microcosm, essentially the place in which one journeys, as the backdrop. Binx, who would have us believe that he is alienated from both the City of God and its negative, has nevertheless read *The City of God*, for in describing his Aunt Emily's husband, Jules Cutrer, he says, "He has made a great deal of money, he has a great many friends, he was Rex of Mardi Gras, he gives freely of himself and his money. He is an exemplary Catholic, but it is hard to know why he takes the trouble. For the world he lives in, the City of Man, is so pleasant that the City of God must hold little in store for him." In the Epilogue, Binx gives us an update: Jules, appropriately enough, suffered a fatal heart attack at the Boston Club, watching the parade on Mardi Gras morning.

And what of Binx? Caught up in rotation while setting about to seduce his latest secretary, Sharon, he jokes, "If I were a Christian, I would make a pilgrimage on foot." But even though he speaks often of the everydayness and the malaise of his life, there are signs that he is well along the road of that pilgrimage. For it is on that road that he is undertaking his "horizontal search" now that he has abandoned the "vertical search" of Platonism just as his mentor Saint Augustine made his own crucial change.

Binx's conversion may be anticipated by the reader who attends to a particular trait of his, if no other. Binx is deeply sensitive to the transitory beauty of New Orleans, its denizens, its flora, its fauna. He is always on the verge of glimpsing the sacramental reality of the visible object. Binx is ready to see the Real Splendor—just as soon as he accepts the grace that will enable him to see.

There is another hint that Binx is but a breath away from commitment: his relationship with his afflicted brother Lonnie. Still intent upon seducing Sharon, Binx takes her to his mother's fishing camp, only to discover that his mother and all his half siblings are there. Quickly forgetting his disappointment, he attends to Lonnie's over a planned movie trip that has fallen through. Binx takes his brothers and sisters to an outdoor movie, placing Lonnie on the hood of the car so that he can loll back and favor his crippled body. Here is the beautiful moment as Binx savors it:

> A good night: Lonnie happy (he looks around at me with the liveliest sense of the secret between us; the secret is that Sharon is not and never will be onto the little touches we see in the movie and, in the seeing, know that the other sees—as when Clint Walker tells the saddle tramp in the softiest [*sic*] easiest old Virginian voice: 'Mister, I don't believe I'd do that if I was you'—Lonnie is beside himself, doesn't know whether to watch Clint Walker or me), this ghost of a theatre, a warm Southern night, the Western Desert and this fine big sweet piece, Sharon.

This scene says volumes about Percy's psychology of intersubjectivity and love. It is also a brilliant reworking of an image from Saint Augustine. In *On Christian Doctrine,* Saint Augustine offers an illustration of what happens to a person who loves God: he is like a theater devotee who is a fan of an actor and loves all other fans of the actor and tries to convert others to fandom. Lonnie *talks* faith to Binx, but it is doubtless his lived faith that succeeds in capturing his older brother.

There is yet a temptation for Binx. Once his aunt condemns him for being thoughtless and unchivalrous about Kate, he lapses into despair, to rail about his "dark pilgrimage" in a world of *merde.* When Kate arrives, though, he takes hope, daring to believe that the black insur-

Houmas House, model for Belle Isle
By permission of Grant L. Robertson

ance salesman who goes into the nearby church has bought insurance not only for New Orleans but also for the City of God. Although Binx poses his statement as a question, he could not conceive of the question without accepting it as the answer: "Is it because he believes that God himself is present here at the corner of Elysian Fields and Bons Enfants? Or is he here for both reasons: through some dim dazzling trick of grace, coming for the one and receiving the other as God's own importunate bonus?" Much earlier, Binx had noted a physical object in the same place, "a schematic sort of bird, the Holy Ghost I suppose." Now, he no longer supposes.

At the end he is prepared to use Saint Augustine as an authority. When Binx's other siblings ask him if their dying crippled brother will on the day of resurrection be able to water-ski, Binx could be citing Chapter XXII of *The City of God* as he assures them that the saved will rise whole. Binx is not the kind of man to lie to children. Binx may be in New Orleans, but he is now on the Bons Enfants side of the street.

There is far less reason to be optimistic about the fate of Lance Lamar, Percy's other protagonist who responds to New Orleans. For he sees nothing but the City of Man. It is of no significance to him that the time is All Souls' Day. Nor is it important to him that his prison is on Annunciation Street, that word *annunciation* naming the event in which the Word was incarnated by the Word.

Lance has read *The City of God*, but all he got out of it was a sexual titillation from Augustine's account of the nuns who were raped by the Visigoths. His reading thus mirrors his obsession with sexuality, which he persists in calling love, in mockery of Percival's constant efforts to get him to acknowledge *agape*. When Lance looks out his cell window at New Orleans, he sees only sex, death, and an obscured sign:

Free &

Ma

B

Again, what he sees is what he is thinking. He thinks that he sees through New Orleans but really does not see New Orleans at all. He has almost none of the responses to the dappledness of the physical world that characterize Binx Bolling. Until he really looks at the world and until he learns from another, Father John, that the sign is not really obscured but like any other symbol is only half visible, awaiting his half to unlock the meaning, he will continue to live in the Earthly City, not New Orleans. He may detour hell, but it will take a miracle.

It seems obvious that, given Percy's fundamental belief, his view of the actual city will not change. To Linda Hobson he said, "In *The Moviegoer,* I was not interested in New Orleans, particularly. What I was interested in was having a conflict, a confrontation of two cultures—the Greco-Roman Stoicism of Binx's father's family and the Roman Catholicism of Binx's mother's family." [7] Percy acknowledged to another interviewer that his original intention in *Lancelot* was to create a dialogue that would contrast the two cities. Lance Lamar was to represent the "Southern Greco-Roman honor code," the Earthly City, and Harry Percival was to represent the "Augustan [*sic*] con-

7. Linda Hobson, "The Study of Consciousness: An Interview with Walker Percy," in *Conversations with Walker Percy,* ed. Lawson and Kramer, 219.

vert," the City of God.[8] Fortunately, Percy abandoned the idea of the colloquy but kept the idea of the two cities. In Percy's New Orleans, a tourist—whether old Ohioan "with a turkey throat and a baseball cap" or Hattiesburg housewife "come down for a day of shopping" or lonely romantic looking in a lingerie window "where black net panties invest legless torsos"—had better be guided more by Saint A than by Triple-A.

8. John F. Baker, "PW Interviews: Walker Percy," *Publishers Weekly,* March 21, 1977, p. 7.

Tennessee Williams
By permission of Richard Freeman Leavitt

South Toward Freedom: Tennessee Williams

W. KENNETH HOLDITCH

In December, 1951, Tennessee Williams accompanied his grandfather, the Reverend Walter Dakin, to New Orleans, where the ninety-four-year-old retired minister wanted to renew acquaintances. It had been almost thirteen years to the day since the playwright had first arrived in the Crescent City, which was to become, to use his oft-repeated phrase, his "spiritual home." During the visit in 1951, the grandfather and grandson stayed at the Monteleone Hotel in the old French Quarter. In *The Rose Tattoo*, which had opened on Broadway exactly one year before, two women discuss their imminent visit to New Orleans for an American Legion convention. When Bessie states that the town is full of excitement and that conventioneers drop paper bags filled with water out of the windows of the Monteleone, her friend Flora responds, "That's an old-fashioned hotel." Bessie replies, "It might be old-fashioned but you'd be surprised at some of the modern up-to-date things that go on there."[1] By contemporary standards, the oldest hotel in the Quarter might have seemed to be outdated to the likes of Bessie and Flora, but it was a landmark with numerous literary associations. Not least, it was at the Monteleone that Arch and Lillie May Persons had been living in 1924 when she gave birth to their son, Truman Streckfus Persons, who later became known to the world as Truman Capote.

Williams liked staying there because from the back rooms on the upper floors he had a view of the Mississippi River. During the 1951 visit, he was at work on *Camino Real*, and after his four or five hours at the typewriter every morning, he and his grandfather would have lunch at some favorite restaurant—Galatoire's, Arnaud's, Maylie's, or Antoine's—and spend the afternoon wandering the Quarter or visiting friends. In a letter the two men wrote together to the author's mother after leaving the city, they related that the hotel's owner had sent a basket of fruit to their rooms to welcome them and that two weeks later, when they checked out, they learned "that we had been his guests the entire time we were there."[2] It seems unlikely that Mr. Monteleone would have accommodated the playwright and the Reverend Mr. Dakin on the basis of the not particularly flattering reference in *The Rose Tattoo*, a play he had probably not seen or read. Four years earlier, however, in 1947, *A Streetcar Named Desire* had premiered in New York, and most literate New Orleanians must have realized the significance of a play that, among other achievements of more importance, had returned New Orleans to a preeminent place on the literary map of America.

One of the most pervasive qualities distinguishing the work of southern novelists, dramatists, and poets is a sense of place, an identification with one specific spot in the world, which happens to be located in the South, from which they draw strength and even their identity as surely as Scarlett O'Hara draws hers from the "good rich earth of

1. Tennessee Williams, *The Theatre of Tennessee Williams* (7 vols.; New York, 1972–75), II, 307.
2. Quoted by Edwina Dakin Williams in *Remember Me to Tom* (New York, 1963), 226–27.

Tara." Eudora Welty has described place as a magical element of fiction, one of the "lesser angels" that watch over the writer, southern or northern, British or European. Consider the Yorkshire moors of Emily Brontë, the Boston and Salem of Nathaniel Hawthorne, the Wessex of Thomas Hardy, the Combray of Marcel Proust, the Macondo of Gabriel García Márquez. With the southern writer, though, place takes on an added dimension and power somehow, given the decided rootedness of most people from the region. Meet a native of the South who has lived in New York, Berlin, or Madrid for twenty or thirty years and ask him where he or she is from, and the response is more likely to be Gadsden, Alabama, or Columbus, Mississippi, than the town or city that has been home in more recent decades. Richard Leavitt recalls, in a very telling anecdote, that one night in the 1970s, after he and Williams slipped into a theater during a special benefit performance of one of Williams' plays, an officious manager, not recognizing the author, challenged them and demanded to know, "Where are you from?" Without hesitation, the author replied, "Mississippi"—this more than half a century after he had left the state of his birth.[3] In no writer is the sense of being rooted in the South, the feeling for place, more sharply delineated than in the relationship between Tennessee Williams and the region. The part of the South with which he came to be most completely identified was not the place of his birth or his growing up but New Orleans, where his creative alter ego in a sense came to life.

In no city in the United States, with the possible exception of New York, is the sense of place stronger and more consequential than in New Orleans, shrouded as this city is in a literary mystique that for many, both residents and outsiders, has replaced the reality. Cleanth Brooks has observed that "New Orleans has become one of the cities of the mind, and is therefore immortal."[4] The image of the most foreign of all North American cities that has for two centuries prevailed in the consciousness of most Americans is largely a result of what authors have written about it. During the Reconstruction era, people

3. Richard Leavitt, conversation with author, March 16, 1989.
4. Cleanth Brooks, conversation with author, September 18, 1977.

63

all over the country became aware of the great diversity of the newly re-United States, and writers of the local-color school strove to satisfy the growing curiosity of readers about unique and hitherto unknown locales. George Washington Cable became the major chronicler of New Orleans, and it was his portrayal of the city that established for several generations of readers an image of a languid, exotic, mysterious, and essentially sinful municipality. Cable's image of the city prevailed into the middle of the twentieth century, and no other writer's work about New Orleans came close to challenging it until Williams' *A Streetcar Named Desire* was staged in 1947. The play's picture of the city is not wholly at odds with that of Cable. The bizarre and foreign elements remain conspicuous, as does the flavor of decadence and immorality—the two writers shared a puritanical background—but Williams was dealing with a period when the Quarter had long ceased to be French as well as with a different segment of the population from that in *Old Creole Days* and *The Grandissimes*.

If *A Streetcar Named Desire* is the play by Williams most shaped by its association with New Orleans and the one that has done the most to create a national image for the city, it is *Vieux Carré*, written and staged thirty years later, that best exemplifies what the playwright felt about his "spiritual home" and its effect on his work. In the stage directions, Williams specifies the time as the "period between winter 1938 and spring 1939" and describes the setting as a barren rooming house that should suggest "all the cheap rooming houses of the world." This one, however, is real and is located at 722 Toulouse Street, "in the Vieux Carré of New Orleans, where it remains standing." In the course of the play, the impoverished Writer ("myself those many years ago") struggles to create literature in a small attic room and works for his landlady in order to pay the rent. In the course of a few months in the city, he loses his virginity to a paratrooper on New Year's Eve, submits to the sexual advances of the tenant in the next room, and for the first time in his life comes face to face with many of the frustrations, disappointments, and injustices of the world. The Writer is haunted by the ghost of his recently deceased grandmother (Mrs. Walter Dakin in real life), who serves, for a time at least, as an influence restraining him from plunging into the dangerous and enticing pool of freedom he has discovered. His painful education, presumably advantageous for an aspiring author who wants to portray reality in his writing, is acknowledged by the protagonist in his words to Mrs. Wire, the landlady, after their return from night court, where she has been fined for pouring boiling water through the floor onto an orgy being staged by her first-floor tenant: "God, but I was ignorant when I came here! This place has been a—I ought to pay you—tuition . . ."⁵

Imagine if you can the French Quarter of the late 1930s, the setting of *Vieux Carré*. The old Creole families, descendants of the French settlers who in 1718 had founded Nouvelle Orleans and then built it up into a great capital of a New World colony, were for the most part gone. An influx of European immigrants, most of them from countries other than France, had converted the old square, thirteen blocks long, six blocks wide, into what could more appropriately have been called an Italian Quarter. The protective watchfulness of the Vieux Carré Commission was a dream of the future harbored by a few pioneer preservationists, and some Creole town houses and other old structures, haunted by past glories, were being torn down without a second thought. In essence, the French Quarter, today recognized by New Orleanians as a priceless heritage, the city's prime tourist attraction, and as a consequence, its major source of revenue, was in that period, just before World War II, little more than a slum. Many an uptown or suburban resident of the city in those days would gladly have seen it bulldozed and replaced by the wonderful monuments to that new god of the twentieth century, Progress. Not surprisingly, the shabby but genteel old village, resistant to modernization, had in the 1920s become a gathering place for writers and artists—a spot, as the playwright described it in *Where I Live*, in which poets "huddle together for some dim, communal comfort."⁶ Here Thomas Lanier Williams found his spiritual home.

When Williams arrived in New Orleans in late December, 1938, in

5. Tennessee Williams, *Vieux Carré* (New York, 1979), 4, 66.
6. Tennessee Williams, *Where I Live: Selected Essays* (New York, 1978), 4.

full flight from St. Louis, he was, to use his own poetic simile, "like a migratory bird going to a more congenial climate."[7] Uprooted at the age of eight from the idyllic childhood he had spent in his grand-parents' homes in various Mississippi towns, Tom, his mother, and his sister, Rose, were dropped down in an alien and to them cold atmosphere, the city of St. Louis. It might as well have been the moon. Edwina Dakin Williams, who as the daughter of an Episcopalian rector had been part of the top social echelon, such as it was, in the provincial South, found herself an outsider, for the name Dakin stirred not a ripple on the surface of St. Louis society and residents of the Deep South were still looked down upon as intrinsically inferior in every regard. The children, accustomed to the attention not only of their mother but also of two doting grandparents, were equally affected. Compounding the problem was the presence of the father, Cornelius Williams, who for the first eight years of Tom's life had been an infrequent intruder into the close-knit family circle, a salesman who seemed to have, like his exemplar in *The Glass Menagerie*, fallen in love with long distance. The peaceful southern idyll was replaced by an unfriendly environment in which domestic squabbles between the proper Miss Edwina and her drinking, gambling husband, who looked upon the sensitivity and creativity of his son as weakness, were regular occurrences. The result of the dislocation and realignment of family relationships upon the children was traumatic. Rose retreated into mental illness, and when Tom fled from St. Louis at the age of twenty-eight, he was fleeing not only the city that had seemed hostile to the child he had been but also everything it represented in terms of home and father—fleeing it and forever finding it, again and again, in the creative microcosm of his work.

When he entered what he later called the "decadent world of New Orleans," he was searching for a number of things: release from life in a city he "loathed"; escape from a painful family situation that stood fair to deprive him of his reason; a job; and a place in which to practice the craft to which he had with his departure from home firmly and irrevocably committed himself. He apparently spent his first night at

7. Tennessee Williams, interview by Eric Paulsen, WWL-TV, New Orleans, April 12, 1982.

the YMCA on Lee Circle and the next day looked up a couple who lived in the French Quarter, Knute and Colette Heldner, to whom he had been directed by friends in St. Louis. Soon he had located his own place, that third-floor room with a dormer window at 722 Toulouse Street, in which if the persona known as Tennessee Williams was not born, he certainly spent the first months of his existence. Those months effected a remarkable conversion: Thomas Lanier Williams, proper young grandson of an Episcopalian rector, was now Tennessee as well. When he first arrived in the Quarter, he recalled many years later, he was "terribly shocked by the Bohemian life. Now it seems my natural ambience." During the remaining forty-three years of his life, the Quarter was a "place where I could catch my breath," where it was possible to write and enjoy the leisurely life of the most foreign North American city.[8] In an interview in 1978 with Don Lee Keith, he observed that the farther South one traveled in the United States, the more compatible life seemed to be,[9] and thus it is not surprising that the two places that shared his allegiance were New Orleans and Key West, the places where the migrating bird came to roost for as long as he was ever able to rest. It was New Orleans, however, that he thought of as home: "If I can be said to have a home, it is in New Orleans where I've lived off and on since 1938 and which has provided me with more material than any other part of the country."[10] The city became an integral part of his work, supplying him with subjects, settings, and symbols. It is the locale of his masterpiece, *A Streetcar Named Desire*, and of two other full-length plays, *Suddenly, Last Summer* and *Vieux Carré*, as well as of numerous one-acts, including *The Lady of Larkspur Lotion* and *Lord Byron's Love Letter*, and of short stories such as "Angel in the Alcove" and "One Arm" and "The Yellow Bird."

What he found during his first stay in the French Quarter alternately charmed and shocked, even repelled, this self-styled puritan: a slum, yes, and yet paradoxically a magical potpourri of sights, sounds,

8. *Ibid.*
9. Tennessee Williams, interview by Don Lee Keith, Theater for the Performing Arts, New Orleans, January 25, 1978.
10. Quoted by Nancy Tischler in *Tennessee Williams: The Rebellious Puritan* (New York, 1961), 62.

and influences unlike anything he had known in small-town Mississippi, in Tennessee or Missouri or Iowa. There were delightful people like the author and bon vivant Lyle Saxon, known as Mr. French Quarter, who soon became his friend; Roark Bradford, whose play *Green Pastures* was a phenomenal Broadway hit; and Olive Leonhardt, a Bohemian artist who was to figure as a character in several of his works. All were individualists who lived not according to the dictates of society but as they pleased in a City That Care Forgot. (A local aphorism has it that New Orleanians don't care what you do but that they do want to know about it.) In addition, the cuisine was extraordinary, the best, he wrote his mother, that he had ever eaten—anywhere other than home, he diplomatically added—and he was delighted by the abundance of inexpensive seafood.[11] At the time, two pounds of shrimp sold in the markets for nine cents, three dozen oysters for only a quarter.

It was not, however, a time of unbridled license and pleasure, and those early stays in the Vieux Carré were not easy for the aspiring dramatist. He was distressed by the mental condition of his beloved sister and by the physical condition and subsequent death of the grandmother he adored. He was impoverished and, since his hopes of obtaining a position with the New Deal Writers' Project were unfulfilled, forced to take a series of jobs for which he was ill suited. He pawned most of his possessions and occasionally was even reduced to the humiliation of begging cigarettes from strangers. Yet an amazing range of experiences was crowded into those few months, and when he left his newfound spiritual home for the first time on his way west, he had truly been metamorphosed by his exposure to the city's strong spirit of place. It was during this period and in this locale that he turned his back on many of his family ties and committed himself completely to his writing, and it was here that he adopted the "Bohemian" life-style that was to mark his existence for the remaining four decades he was to live. Interestingly, in 1941 he was back again, this time not fleeing the stifling atmosphere of St. Louis and painful family relation-

11. Edwina Dakin Williams, *Remember Me*, 99–100.

ships but seeking congenial surroundings to restore his spirits, wounded by the failure of *Battle of Angels,* his first commercially produced play.

Several written versions of what happened during those early stays—the *Memoirs,* letters to his mother, poems, short stories, one-act plays, *Vieux Carré,* diaries, and interviews—attest that the city worked a remarkable transformation in turning the young puritan gentleman into something of a confirmed hedonist. Williams was not the first to observe and comment upon the Latin laxity in morality and ethical standards that has always been integral to southern Louisiana. Justin Kaplan states that when Walt Whitman came to New Orleans in 1848 it had acquired a reputation as the "wickedest city in Christendom." [12] A decade after Whitman's visit, Frederick Law Olmsted related the story of a young New England family man who, after working briefly in the city, became a drunkard—a common occurrence, he said, among boys "who had been 'too carefully brought up at home' when they came to New Orleans." [13] Although Williams later professed shock when he first observed the more or less public actions of homosexuals in the Quarter, which has always been one of the most liberal spots in the United States with respect to sexual freedom, it was here, according to his own account, that he lost his virginity. (It happened on New Year's Eve, he stated in an interview in 1928, but his biographers do not agree on the exact date of his belated discovery and acknowledgment of what he termed a "certain flexible quality in my sexual nature," a "duality of gender.") [14] Like Alma Tutwiler of "The Yellow Bird," he seems to have learned early that "you didn't have to go into a good-time house to have a good time in New Orleans," and within a few years, he had overcome his first reaction and become an active part of the gay community.

From 1938 to 1983, he lived in a succession of places in New

12. Justin Kaplan, *Walt Whitman: A Life* (New York, 1980), 139.

13. Frederick Law Olmsted, "Men and Manners," in *The World from Jackson Square,* ed. Etiola S. Basso (New York, 1948), 165.

14. Tennessee Williams, interview by Eric Paulsen, WWL-TV, New Orleans, April 12, 1982.

The streetcar named Desire
By permission of the Historic New Orleans Collection

Orleans, from the Toulouse Street attic and a roach-infested criblike room on Bourbon Street to the elegant Pontchartrain Hotel to the quaint and charming Maison de Ville to, finally, his own house on Dumaine Street. In an apartment on St. Peter Street from which he could hear day and night "that rattletrap streetcar that bangs through the Quarter, up one old street and down another," he completed *A Streetcar Named Desire* in 1946. He concluded his *Memoirs* with words about the Dumaine Street house that he bought in the early 1960s: "I hope to die in my sleep, when the time comes, and I hope it will be in the beautiful big brass bed in my New Orleans apartment." [15] Unfortunately, his death in a New York hotel was far from the congenial South he had loved and far from the city that had inspired him.

The words that best represent Williams' attitude toward New Orleans are obviously *Bohemia* and *freedom*. If St. Louis represented for him captivity, as symbolized by the confinement of Amanda, Laura, and Tom in an unpleasant cul-de-sac in a northern city in *The Glass*

15. Tennessee Williams, *Memoirs* (Garden City, N.Y., 1975), 248.

Menagerie, New Orleans seems to have represented a degree of liberty he had never dreamed existed. He expressed his reaction in an interview in 1969: "I think I felt a sense of freedom when I came to New Orleans. Freedom is always something I've sought above anything else. My greatest instinct is to be free. I found that in New Orleans, and it certainly was a great impetus to me as a writer."[16] By *freedom* he surely meant that Latin attitude which has always been a component of the city's life. For 250 years authors have commented—some with delight, others with censure—on New Orleans' languid, lazy, laissez-faire approach to religion, business, politics, law enforcement, labor, intellectual pursuits, and sexuality.

In the life and work of Williams, however, that freedom was not all sweetness and light, not merely some Isadora Duncan dance of the spirit; and the continuing ambivalence, the struggle within him between the intrinsic puritanism he professed and the freedom he embraced, is exemplified by what happens to the characters in his New Orleans plays and stories. Sometimes freedom degenerates into a rather dank, even gross, license and disorderliness, as in the destruction of perhaps his greatest character, Blanche DuBois, who in a sense falls victim to it. Her flight to this city is, ironically, a flight into the powerful and destructive arms of her enemies in a place where the threat of death is ever present—in the chant of the street vendor ("Flores para los muertos"), in the Cemeteries streetcar line, which intersects the one named Desire—a place where the animal passions inherent in human nature are unleashed in the person of Stanley and his poker-playing cronies. In view of what happens to Blanche, one of Stella's lines earlier in the play—"New Orleans is not like other cities"—takes on an ominous and foreboding burden.

In the New Orleans one-act plays and short stories, several other women come to the end of hope and encounter violence and even destruction: Mrs. Hardwicke-Moore, the "lady" of *The Lady of Larkspur Lotion,* awaits in vain a check from her Brazilian rubber plantation; the Old Woman and the Spinster in *Lord Byron's Love Letter*

16. Tennessee Williams, interview by Don Lee Keith, Theater for the Performing Arts, New Orleans, 1969.

live in poverty, fed on dreams and an occasional pittance tourists pay to see the relic that is their only treasure; Mrs. Wire in *Vieux Carré* is a bitter, half-crazed harridan who has lost her son and turns her anger against her tenants, among whom are two elderly ladies from once-prominent families who have been reduced to living on food from garbage cans. Tye, a Bourbon Street barker in *Vieux Carré*, relates a horrifying tale to his lover, Jane, about the stripper known as the Champagne Girl: when she quit sleeping with the boss of organized crime, he unleashed attack dogs that tore her to bits. Male characters often fare no better in their relationship to the city. In *Orpheus Descending*, Val Xavier flees New Orleans, where he has been confined to a life of providing sexual "entertainment" for a certain circle of men in the Quarter. The protagonist of the short story "One Arm" turns to prostitution to support himself, and the quick-sketch artist Nightingale, dying of tuberculosis, is shipped off to a charity hospital by the landlady who wants to get him out of her house.

The portrayal of Williams' spiritual home in his works is multi-faceted, not only in the attitudes he expressed but also in his choice of neighborhoods and characters. There is the Quarter, of course, one of the "last frontiers of Bohemia" as he called it, the setting of *A Streetcar Named Desire, Vieux Carré*, and numerous shorter works, but there is also uptown, or the American sector, which came to represent for him the life that Edwina Williams had aspired to and that she wanted for her children, the life of money and privilege and the social position he had rejected in embracing the Bohemian life-style. After he entertained a group of uptown debutantes and their dates in 1946, he wrote that they had been shocked by his living arrangements with a young flamenco dancer and that, as a result, "I am told that my name is mentioned only in whispers in mixed company."[17] Thirty years later he was to recall that episode in his *Memoirs* with amusement, observing that his exclusion from "polite society" had surely been for the best, since his place was Bohemia: "I love to visit the other side now and

17. Donald Windham, ed., *Tennessee Williams' Letters to Donald Windham, 1940–1965* (New York, 1977), 182.

Williams' house in the French Quarter
Courtesy of W. Kenneth Holditch

then, but on my social passport Bohemia is indelibly stamped, without regret on my part." [18] It might be argued that several years after his encounter with the straitlaced and snobbish young New Orleans socialites, he executed a sweet revenge in the two plays that make up *Garden District: Suddenly, Last Summer* and *Something Unspoken.* In them life in uptown New Orleans is portrayed as desperate, life-denying, even carnivorous. Life in the French Quarter might present problems for its residents, but at least they were alive, they were survivors, and they were concerned with something more than social reputations, making debuts, being regents of the Daughters of Runnymede, or printing one poem a year on an antique press.

Whatever excesses might result from the atmosphere and license of life in New Orleans, however, the young Williams in the years 1938–

18. Tennessee Williams, *Memoirs,* 100.

1941, charmed by the Quarter as generations of writers before him had been, found it an environment in which his suppressed creative and sexual yearnings could come to the surface and be openly acknowledged and expressed. Late in life he remarked that more than half his best work had been written in the city. The evidence of the printed word is more than sufficient to show that New Orleans effected a conversion in the character of Tennessee Williams. But what did he make of the conversion? That he became America's premier playwright surely owes much to the energizing freedom he found in a place where he could be himself. Truly the flight from St. Louis back toward the South of his youth, painful as the reasons motivating it were for the dramatist, proved in the passage of time to be one of the most fortunate journeys in the history of American literature.

To call Williams a regionalist because of his use of New Orleans and other parts of the South as settings would be to ignore the universality of his vision of human life. Metaphorically, a woman or a man could ride the streetcar named Desire, transfer to one called Cemeteries, and get off at Elysian Fields any time in human history, anywhere in the world. Only in the South, however, could the components so combine, since only there exists the one triangular plot of earth—of which Laurel, Mississippi, is one point, New Orleans another, and the creative imagination of Tennessee Williams the third—on which could live the only Blanche DuBois. Without New Orleans, *A Streetcar Named Desire* could never have been exactly the masterpiece it became. (An earlier version of the play, set in St. Louis, was entitled "The Poker Night." One can only imagine what would have been lost had the playwright not discovered the ideal location and major symbol for his story.) Without New Orleans, much of his great work would not have been quite the same, marked as it is by that magical sense of the most unusual of southern locales.

The relationship between Tennessee Williams and New Orleans, then, was for forty-five years a symbiotic one. The city fed him inspiration, and he repaid her more than amply by putting her name permanently on the literary map of America. Without Tennessee Williams, New Orleans would not be quite the place it is today. Shortly after the success of *A Streetcar Named Desire*, a friend remarked to him that for the rest of his life there would never be a night when that play was not being performed somewhere in the world. That prophecy proved to be true, and the work continues to be performed regularly in theaters all over the world. Every time the curtain goes up on the magic of that modern tragedy, whether in New York or London or Moscow, in St. Paul or Dallas or Miami, in a production professional or amateur, the New Orleans of the mind comes alive for new audiences and new generations of playgoers.

Jackson Square
Courtesy of the State Library of Louisiana

New Orleans as a Literary Center: Some Problems

LEWIS P. SIMPSON

When we look at the great historical centers of modern literature in Europe—London, Paris, Vienna, Rome, Madrid—we must of course conclude that no similar center exists, or has existed, in the United States or, for that matter, anywhere in any nation belonging to the two continents of the New World that came into history in the fifteenth century. The reason is not far to seek. No city in the New World has a direct historical continuity with the origin of the modern sensibility of literary order, for that developed in twelfth- and fifteenth-century Europe when the two medieval realms of order, state and church (the latter had incorporated the order of the clerks, the men of letters), became three—the realms of church, of state, and of secular letters and learning—and cities that had been religious centers became also centers of secular thought. In the colonial world that would become the republic of the United States, the religious impulse in the founding of cities in the wilderness soon yielded to the dynamic secular city as a center of commerce. In America, the idea of the secular city as a city of letters—as Paris or London had become when the primacy of religion declined—was distinctly secondary. But it was not entirely absent. A residue of cultural piety was expressed in the naming of raw American settlements London or Paris—or frequently, was very directly expressed in naming embryonic towns Athens, the reference being to the Athens of Plato, Aristotle, and Aeschylus, a pagan city that had survived the collapse of ancient civilization to become the prototypical Western city of mind and letters. Nor was not being named Athens a bar to the identification of an American city with the ancient city-state of Pericles. The Boston of Lowell, Holmes, Longfellow, and Emerson, as the "Athens of America," more than any other city of the nation fulfilled the three requisites of the modern city of letters: that it have publishers and a commerce in books; that it possess a concentration of literary and intellectual energy sufficient to sustain an active, and at times an intense, literary life; and that it be a city with enough historical depth and contemporary variety to be itself the subject of poets and storytellers. At the same time that Boston was being celebrated as Athens reborn, New York was on its way to becoming in the postbellum United States a city of letters far removed from the image of Athens—a metropolitan, and monopolistic, marketplace of letters, at once singularly American and singularly international in character. William Dean Howells left Boston for New York in 1890, believing that the Athens of America was no longer the literary center of the nation, for it no longer reflected its reality, which had become that of a sprawling, pluralistic, capitalistic society. Although his expectations of New York City were not entirely fulfilled, as some of his later writings indicate—*Literary Friends and Acquaintance,* in particular, was devoted to memorializing the Boston ideal—Howells' prophetic feeling that New York would become the dominant city on the American literary scene was right. Philadelphia, the only antebellum competitor with New York besides Boston, faded from the literary scene after the war. In the early twentieth century the major heartland city, Chicago, made its bid to be the literary capital of the nation but could not sustain its ambition, although it did better than San Francisco in the 1960s, when it seemed for an illusory moment that American letters might begin to center in the City Lights Bookstore. A hundred years after the author of *A Hazard of New Fortunes* hazarded his own fortunes in New York, that city is still the American literary center—even though by the end of the 1950s the concentration of mind and letters in New York had become comparatively marginal and by the end of the 1980s New York publishing had largely been swallowed up by giant corporations in the process of diversification and merger.

But what of the cities, as the idiom of another day put it, at the South? By their own historic definition of themselves in the 1860s as cities of another nation—even though their citizens thought they were the true nation established in 1789—the southern cities had ruled out the possibility that any one of them could in any foreseeable future become a national literary center. Indeed they had ruled out this possibility before the Secession through their integral association with not only the perpetuation but the expansion of an American slave society. At once uniquely modern in its self-defined literary character and uniquely alienated from the historical age in which it existed and in which it was doomed to destruction, this society, feeling itself increasingly threatened, demanded and for the most part secured not merely the loyalty but the active support of its men of letters. The *Southern Literary Messenger,* in Richmond, Virginia, and the *Southern Literary Quarterly,* in Charleston, South Carolina, both began with the aspiration to become national magazines but became instead organs of southern opinion. The city of Charleston, most prominently represented by the energetic editor and novelist William Gilmore Simms, was as close as the antebellum South came to having a literary center.

Meanwhile, after the War of 1812, New Orleans—a growing, affluent port situated in what could be reckoned the most favorable place for a port in the new nation, just above the terminus of its vast heartland river system in the Gulf of Mexico, which afforded an unimpeded seaway to the Caribbean Sea and the Atlantic Ocean—emerged as a key American city. With its population of French, Spanish, Anglo-Saxon, African, and West Indian elements, New Orleans had a more colorful and complex culture than any other American city. Its differences enhanced by its almost universal subscription to the Roman

Catholic faith, it obviously seemed to offer great possibilities as a literary center.

One reason, possibly the overriding one, that New Orleans did not like Richmond and Charleston at least take on the semblance of a literary center is that in the critical years of the city's first great expansion, between the War of 1812 and the Civil War, literary aspiration was completely obscured by the city's obsessive ambition to become a great national and international marketplace. The literary situation of New Orleans may be pointedly illustrated by two events in the antebellum history of periodical publication in America. One is that a year after David Whitaker founded the *Southern Quarterly Review* in New Orleans in 1841 as an expression of his faith in the city's literary potential, he moved his magazine to Charleston, where it drew sufficient support to continue publication for the next fourteen years, a long run for antebellum periodicals in the South. The second is the establishment of the *Commercial Review of the South and West* in New Orleans in 1846 by a young Charlestonian, J. B. D. De Bow, who, after a quarrel with the editor of the *Southern Quarterly Review* over his role as a contributor, had come to the Crescent City fired up with a vision of the economic possibilities of the South. This vision replaced one he had had of the South's literary possibilities when he was a delegate to the Southern Commercial Convention in Memphis in 1845. Emphasizing the commercial focus of his journal, which soon became known as *De Bow's Review,* the editor and publisher assured his readers that its utilitarian intention would not be compromised by an undue interest in literature. Dedicated to a "fair exposition of the character which literature will assume when it is pressing up amid a toiling people," the literary department would be restricted to "biographical sketches of distinguished, practical, and business men, of public benefactors, and high-reaching directors and controllers of a struggling age." The only other offerings of a literary nature in *De Bow's Review* would be articles dealing with "developments in the book-trade."[1] Thus the young

1. Paul S. Passkoff and David J. Wilson, eds., *The Cause of the South: Selections from De Bow's Review* (Baton Rouge, 1982), 14.

Charlestonian who had in his native city begun a career in which he would have devoted himself to classical literature, history, and philosophy became in New Orleans the influential editor of the most successful commercial journal in the antebellum South. *De Bow's Review* projected an image of New Orleans that was a distinct influence on its development as a commercial center and port, where on an average day four hundred steamboats were docked and the Cotton Kingdom transacted a considerable portion of its business. Well after the war, as Mark Twain says in *Life on the Mississippi,* New Orleans continued to be the metropolis of the South.

This is not to suggest that antebellum New Orleans had no literary life. I think it is possible to say, however, that had the South won the Civil War, the city might never have developed an appreciable literary image. But after the surrender—when the Confederacy became at a stroke the Old Confederacy and the South the Old South, and the aura of a never-never-land exoticism began to spread over the land of the Lost Cause—New Orleans in the guise of *Old* New Orleans became the leading presence of that form of nineteenth-century literary exoticism known as local color.

In an excellent essay, Thomas Richardson refers to the observation by the northern journalist Edward King when he visited New Orleans in 1873 that here was the "battle" of a "picturesque and unjust civilization of the past with a prosaic and leveling civilization of the present." The literary interpretation of this conflict in George Washington Cable, Grace King, Alice Dunbar-Nelson, Lafcadio Hearn, and Kate Chopin justifies, Richardson says, Warner Berthoff's contention that in the last three decades of the nineteenth century there was a New Orleans literary renaissance. But in spite of the rich competition of past and present in New Orleans—marked, as Richardson points out, by "creole versus American, black versus white, traditional versus progressive values"—only two works now seem distinctly to represent major achievements in the later-nineteenth-century period: Cable's *The Grandissimes* and Chopin's *The Awakening.* If a reason is sought for the literary slightness of New Orleans, a chief clue no doubt lies in Edward King's perception that the slave society of the antebellum city

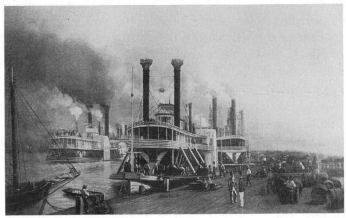

Steamboats at the dockside, from a painting by Hippolyte Victor Valentin Sebron, 1853
Courtesy of the State Library of Louisiana

represented a "picturesque and unjust civilization."[2] The yoking of the adjectives *picturesque* and *unjust* suggests the essential superficiality, or naïveté, of the local-color response to the literary potential of New Orleans—of, for that matter, a good deal of the local-color movement in America, especially in the South. What might be called the local-color syndrome has been the source of both the literary recognition of New Orleans and its literary damnation. Perhaps I speak too grandly and should say merely of its literary ineffectuality. In any event, I am thinking not so much of the failure of New Orleans to become a publishing center—that was never in the cards—as of its failure to develop a complex and energetic literary life and its failure to become a setting of variety and complexity for the literary imagination.

One way to look at the literary history of New Orleans is to see it as a process wherein the literary imagination isolated the Vieux Carré as the only interesting setting in the city, thereby reducing the whole expanding city to one of its small parts. The literary history of New Orleans is in its general context one facet of the literary colonization of the South, a phenomenon that, like the economic colonization of the

2. Thomas Richardson, "Local Color in Louisiana," in *The History of Southern Literature*, ed. Louis D. Rubin, Jr., *et al.* (Baton Rouge, 1985), 199.

81

South by the North, was inherent in the situation of the South as an exporter of raw materials to manufacturers in the North and abroad. Largely dependent on northern sources of book production and distribution before the Civil War, southern authors found themselves still more dependent after the conflict. Ironically, their dependence was proportionately greater, for they had more to export, having found that there was a growing national market for romantic stories by southern authors about the Old South and the War, and about a romanticized contemporary South. No product the southern writers turned out, moreover, was more eminently exportable than a story set in the city that even before the war had attracted attention as the most exotic of the South. Now, through an image nurtured by a whole group of writers—Cable, Chopin, Lafcadio Hearn, Grace King, Ruth McEnery Stuart—New Orleans unquestionably afforded the most exotic setting, rural or urban, in the whole nation.

By the beginning of the twentieth century the local-color damnation of New Orleans was so complete that it was virtually impossible for the imagination to transcend it. The attraction of writers and artists to the Vieux Carré in the 1920s promised far more than it yielded, and the Quarter's bid to become a southern Greenwich Village—which for a time was backed up by a few writers of genuine talent but never by a genuine congregation—ended with Lyle Saxon and Roark Bradford. Somewhat later, in the wake of the Second World War, the literary imagination did appear to shift toward the subversion of local-color New Orleans. Nelson Algren's notorious *A Walk on the Wild Side,* for instance, seemed to offer the New Orleans of bald reality. The shift had been anticipated as early as 1935 in Faulkner's bizarre novel *Pylon.* Set in New Orleans—called New Valois in the novel—this seamy story, containing many echoes of T. S. Eliot's *The Waste Land,* involves a New Orleans newsman and daredevil pilots who pursue the highly lethal career of racing tiny airplanes over a course marked by pylons. Yet what at first appeared to be the subversion of local colorism by a mode of fierce novelistic realism has proved to be simply an inversion of the genteel local-color image into a local-color image of exotic depravity. New Orleans defies its own reality.

Is New Orleans ever to be redeemed from its imprisonment in the exotic mode? Not of course if the national tourism industry—eagerly abetted by the city and state tourism bureaus—or the national literary industry can help it. Whether or not the economic, political, and literary colonization of the South as a whole has ended is arguable, but it is obvious that the literary colonization of Louisiana, and certainly of New Orleans, continues.

My view, I realize, is eminently open to challenge; and I have challenged it myself as being the outrageous result of vacuous theorizing about literary history. Even so, I have come up with no more than two authors since the days of Cable and Chopin who seems to me convincingly to redeem New Orleans from exoticism. I refer, as you must logically guess, to Walker Percy and John Kennedy Toole.

The case that may be made for Percy and Toole as redeemers of Nouvelle Orleans is too complex to be treated summarily; I here hope only to make a suggestion or two with respect to the image of New Orleans in Percy's *The Moviegoer* and in Toole's *A Confederacy of Dunces*.

The Moviegoer (1961) has often been interpreted in terms of its exemplification of the existentialist quest for meaning, without much attention to its setting. At other times it has been interpreted as a novel in which the setting is appropriate to the formulaic theme of the standard southern novel: tradition embattled with change. But Percy, in employing the New Orleans setting in this, his first novel, significantly fuses the motive of the existentialist quest and the New Orleans setting. The story of Binx Bolling's quest for meaning is integral with its setting. Percy does not repudiate the New Orleans of the Vieux Carré in favor of the New Orleans of Gentilly. In his poetic treatment of the city, he recognizes that Gentilly is not like a suburb of Houston or Los Angeles but is a section of the fabled city that has—with what degree of desperation—epitomized itself as the City That Care Forgot, or more recently and more vulgarly, as the Big Easy, thus obliquely relating itself to the hard ideal of New York City, the Big Apple. In contemplating Percy's sense of New Orleans as the setting of *The Moviegoer,* one finds oneself thinking about Tennessee Williams' achievement in *A Streetcar Named Desire* in transmuting the exotic aura of the French Quarter into the tragic aura that hovers about the story of what history has made of that perishing flower of the Old South, Blanche DuBois.

In one of the earlier interviews, Percy said of *The Moviegoer*, "So many people ask me why I didn't write about the French Quarter in New Orleans instead of Gentilly. Gentilly looks like any other place. All the alienated writers say it is anonymous. Well, that's what my main character, Binx Bolling, likes about it. He likes the quality of the sky out there in Gentilly. He likes the parochial school across the street, made of brick and aluminum and glass."[3] Taking this statement at face value, one may wonder why Percy did not choose to locate Binx in a suburb in Houston or Los Angeles—in some place that truly looks like any other place—instead of in a suburb that, no matter how different it may be from the Vieux Carré, is within the general ambience of the literary image of New Orleans. The reason he did not is that his sensibility of alienation—although it conforms, as he insists, to the orthodox Christian conception of alienation—is governed too by that ironic subtle stress characteristic of the sophisticated southern writer, whose mind, attuned to the contextual nuances of American history and of the history of the South in particular, harbors not simply the memory of the experience but the experience of the memory of belonging to a nation that originated as a series of remote imperial colonies (usually referred to as plantations) strung up and down the Atlantic seaboard and backed up against a vast continental wilderness.

This experience of the meaning of colonization, and subsequently of revolution and independence—of, to put it another way, irrevocable alienation from a homeland—has informed all American writing. As the experience has moved to the margins of awareness, it has been transmuted into the progressively more ineffable experience of memory alienated by history. Percy's achievement, both more subtle and more comprehensive than Williams', is suggested to the imagination of the reader by the way he extends, though with no contrived intention, the run of Williams' streetcar to the broad avenue, so evocatively

3. Carlton Cremeens, "Walker Percy, the Man and the Novelist: An Interview," in *Conversations with Walker Percy*, ed. Lewis A. Lawson and Victor A. Kramer (Jackson, Miss., 1985), 26.

named, that crosses the city almost from the Vieux Carré to Lake Pontchartrain, Elysian Fields. This goes by the school of "brick and aluminum and glass" where Kate teaches, and Binx at the beginning of the thirty-first year of his "dark pilgrimage on earth" sits on the school playground reflecting that "ninety-eight percent" of men "believe in God," and yet "men are dead, dead, dead." On this "gloomy day," as Binx puts it, Gentilly "is swept fitfully by desire" from the "burning swamp" that edges the area. "Nothing remains of me," he says, "but desire and desire comes howling down Elysian Fields like a mistral. My search has been abandoned; it is no match for my aunt, her rightness and her despairing of men and her despairing of herself."[4]

A *Confederacy of Dunces* resembles *The Moviegoer* in that it too represents the triumph of vision and art over the demands of local color and hence redeems New Orleans from the image of a meretricious exoticism. In an introduction to Toole's story—which was finally published more than a decade after the suicide of its youthful author—Percy observes that it belongs to the realm of *commedia* or tragicomedy. This judgment applies equally well to *The Moviegoer;* at the same time the judgment implies a significant distinction between Percy's own first novel, which since its original publication has become a contemporary classic, and Toole's only novel, which since 1980, when it was brought out by Louisiana State University Press, has also acquired a kind of classic status. The chief measure of that distinction lies in the difference between the leading figures in the two novels, and this difference is in the essential relationship that each figure bears to New Orleans.

Binx and Ignatius are in an exilic relationship to what is ostensibly the same city, but the New Orleans of Binx's displacement is different from that of Ignatius. On the one hand, Ignatius—a "mad Oliver Hardy, a fat Don Quixote, a perverse Thomas Aquinas," Percy calls him; an "intellectual ideologue, deadbeat, goof-off, glutton"—is in "violent revolt against the entire modern age." He "lies in his flannel nightshirt in a back bedroom on Constantinople Street in New Orleans," where "between gigantic seizures of flatulence and eructa-

4. Walker Percy, *The Moviegoer* (New York, 1961), 228.

John Kennedy Toole

tions," he fills "dozens of Big Chief tablets with invective."[5] Binx Bolling, on the other hand, goes daily from a pleasant house on Elysian Fields in Gentilly to the Gentilly financial house of Cutrer, Klostermann & Lejier, where he is employed as a stock and bond broker. Binx describes the building occupied by his firm as a "little bit of old New England with a Creole flavor": the building boasts, he says, a "Parthenon facade" recently added at a cost of twelve thousand dollars but well worth it, "commissions having doubled" since.[6] Binx, in other words, derives from a New Orleans culture that has its origins in the mercantile ambitions associated with Boston, the great American port of the North Atlantic civilization and as such—until it was superseded by New York—the most important agency in the spread of this civilization into the American colonies and eventually into the Mississippi Valley. But since the port of the American heartland, New Or-

5. Walker Percy, Foreword to *A Confederacy of Dunces*, by John Kennedy Toole (Baton Rouge, 1980), vi.
6. Percy, *The Moviegoer*, 72.

leans, opened to the world through the Gulf of Mexico, its destiny was to lie in its connections not with the ports of the North Atlantic but with the exotic ports of the Caribbean and Mediterranean. Binx is not unaware of this. Commenting on the character of his Aunt Emily, whose home is on aristocratic St. Charles Avenue and who lives the life of the antique southerner as Stoic philosopher (she is a figure reminiscent of William Alexander Percy), Binx says that she imagines Uncle Jules as the "Creole Cato," when he is plainly "a canny Cajun straight from Bayou Lafourche, as canny as a Marseilles merchant and a very good fellow but not Cato." Aunt Emily, Binx reflects, joins "all the stray bits and pieces of the past, all that is feckless and gray about people . . . in an unmistakable visage of the heroic or the craven, the noble or the ignoble."[7] Living in the illusion of her capacity to reembody Roman moralism, Aunt Emily provides a foil to Binx's anxious quest for meaning in a world alienated from the possibility of transcendent meaning, either metaphysical or moral. But Ignatius—whose mother is sustained in life by the suspicion that nearly everybody besides herself is a "communiss" and who writes pamphlets with titles like *Is Your Neighbor Really an American?*—belongs to the polyglot New Orleans that Ignatius obliquely identifies when he describes the attraction of the city as being that of a "comfortable metropolis which has a certain apathy and stagnation which I find inoffensive." Although he observes that the climate is mild "here in the Crescent City" and that "I am assured of having a roof over my head and a Dr. Nut in my stomach," he adds that "certain sections of North Africa (Tangiers, etc.) have from time to time excited" his "interest."[8] To make Ignatius' New Orleans more explicitly clear to the reader, Toole employs as an epigraphic reference for his hero's attitude toward the city a quotation from A. J. Liebling's remarkable portrait of Earl Long, *The Earl of Louisiana:* "New Orleans resembles Genoa or Marseilles, or Beirut or the Egyptian Alexandria more than it does New York, although all seaports resemble one another more than they can any place in the interior. Like Havana and Port-au-Prince, New Orleans is within the orbit of a Hellenistic world that never touched the North Atlantic. The

7. *Ibid.*, 49.
8. Toole, *A Confederacy of Dunces,* 103–104.

Mediterranean, Caribbean and Gulf of Mexico form a homogeneous, though interrupted, sea."[9]

Even so, New Orleans is not Tangiers or Genoa or Marseilles; it is not even Havana or Port-au-Prince, though it may resemble the latter places more closely than it does New York. As New Orleans is the memory of Boston and London and Paris, it is at the same time the memory of Tangiers and Marseilles. Ignatius lives in alienation from the memory of what we might call the non-Vergilian Mediterranean culture.

Yet both Binx and Ignatius are conceived as representing an alienation from the memory of the overarching culture of Christendom. Percy and Toole suggest, it seems to me, possibly more than any other writers who have employed the New Orleans setting, the fundamental reason that the American literary imagination has insisted on the colonization of the exotic in this city—on making New Orleans, in the generic meaning of the term *exotic,* a place "outside" the national cultural norm. The essence of the American literary imagination of the colonial experience, and more deeply, the essence of the American literary imagination of the modern historical experience (of which the colonial is the initial phase), is the imagination of the geographical and, more profoundly, the psychic, displacement occasioned by an event roughly contemporary with the discovery of America, that is to say, the destruction of Christendom, and with it the exotic worlds beyond the world, the "outside" worlds of heaven and hell. The meaning of the alienation by history of the memory of those transcendent worlds is at the deeper levels a part of the American experience of history. Percy's and Toole's dramatization of New Orleans as a microcosmic representation of this experience, I realize, may be more readily discernible to southerners. More than any other Americans they yet live in the anxiety of an unresolved tension between memory and history; this is to say, they still live in the historical actuality of the modern world rather than in the illusion of a "postmodern" world.

9. A. J. Liebling, *The Earl of Louisiana* (New York, 1961), 87.

CONTRIBUTORS

ROBERT BUSH, professor emeritus of English, Lehman College, CUNY, was born in Roseland, N.J. Educated at Princeton (A.B., 1938), Columbia (M.A., 1949), and the University of Iowa (Ph.D., 1957), he has also taught at the University of Virginia, Louisiana State University, the Citadel, and Hunter College, CUNY. In both his dissertation "Louisiana Prose Fiction, 1870–1900" (1957) and a series of articles, he has attempted to revive interest in neglected southern authors such as Kate Chopin, Richard Malcolm Johnston, Alice French, Ruth McEnery Stuart, and Grace King. He discovered William Gilmore Simms's comic novel *Paddy McGann* and coedited it as the first volume of the Simms Centennial Edition. He has edited *Grace King of New Orleans: A Selection of Her Writings* (1973) and has written her biography, *Grace King: A Southern Destiny* (1983), which was awarded the General L. Kemper Williams Prize in history by the Louisiana Historical Association, as well as the Louisiana Library Association's literary award for 1984.

W. KENNETH HOLDITCH, research professor of English at the University of New Orleans, was educated at Southwestern University at Memphis (B.A., 1955) and the University of Mississippi (M.A., 1957; Ph.D., 1961). He is the founding publisher and editor of the *Tennessee Williams Journal* and has published short stories, poems, and essays on Faulkner, Williams, Lillian Hellman, and other southern writers. He has created and conducts literary tours of New Orleans.

LEWIS LAWSON, professor of English at the University of Maryland, is a native of Bristol, Tennessee. He was educated at East Tennessee State University (B.S., 1957; M.A., 1959) and the University of

Wisconsin (Ph.D., 1964). Since 1963, he has taught southern literature at the University of Maryland, with time out for Fulbrights in Denmark and Belgium. He is the author of *Another Generation* (1984), *Following Percy* (1988), and *Wheeler's Last Raid* (1986), a Civil War campaign narrative. He is the editor of *Kierkegaard's Presence in Contemporary American Life* (1971) and is the co-editor of *The Added Dimension: The Art and Life of Flannery O'Connor* (1966) and *Conversations with Walker Percy* (1985).

ALICE HALL PETRY, associate professor of English at the Rhode Island School of Design, was born in Hartford, Connecticut. She received her degrees from the University of Connecticut (B.S., 1973), Connecticut College (M.A., 1976), and Brown University (Ph.D., 1979). She was a University scholar at the University of Connecticut and has been a Fulbright scholar in Brazil (1985), a visiting professor of American literature at the University of Colorado at Boulder (1987), and a senior postdoctoral fellow of the American Council of Learned Societies (1987–1988). A specialist in southern literature, short fiction, and women writers and gender issues, she has published in journals like *American Literature, Studies in American Fiction,* and the *Southern Literary Journal,* and is the author of several books: *A Genius in His Way* (1988), on George Washington Cable's 1879 short story collection *Old Creole Days; Fitzgerald's Craft of Short Fiction* (1989); and *Understanding Anne Tyler* (1990). She has edited *Critical Essays on Anne Tyler* (1992). In 1991, she made a lecture tour of Japan under the auspices of the United States Information Agency.

HEPHZIBAH ROSKELLY, assistant professor at the University of North Carolina at Greensboro, has taught rhetoric and composition, and American literature, there since 1989. Born in Dayton, Ohio, she was educated at Murray State University, Kentucky (B.A., 1969), and the University of Louisville (M.A., 1980; Ph.D., 1985). She has directed the University of Louisville's Writing Center, and she later taught for four years at the University of Massachusetts at Boston. She is coauthor of *An Unquiet Pedagogy* (1991) and is coeditor of *Farther Along: Transforming Dichotomies in Rhetoric and Com-*

position (1990). At work on a book on romantic rhetoric, she is also beginning a study of C. S. Peirce and rhetorical theory.

ANNE ROWE, professor of English at Florida State University, teaches American literature, including courses in southern literature. She was educated at Florida State University (B.A., 1967) and the University of North Carolina at Chapel Hill (M.A., 1969; Ph.D., 1973). Her publications include *The Enchanted Country: Northern Writers in the South, 1865–1910* (1978), *The Idea of Florida in the American Literary Imagination* (1986), and articles on Kate Chopin, André Dubus, and regionalism. She is at present working on a book on southern women writers.

LEWIS P. SIMPSON, Boyd Professor Emeritus and William A. Read Professor of English Literature Emeritus at Louisiana State University, and editor emeritus of the *Southern Review,* is the author of *The Man of Letters in New England and the South* (1973), *The Dispossessed Garden: Pastoral and History in Southern Literature* (1975), and *The Brazen Face of History* (1980). His book *Mind and the American Civil War: A Meditation on Lost Causes* (1989) was awarded the 1990 Avery O. Craven Award of the Organization of American Historians. He has edited several volumes, including *The Federalist Literary Mind* (1962) and *The Possibilities of Order: Cleanth Brooks and His Work* (1975), and has coedited, with Louis D. Rubin, Jr., and others, *The History of Southern Literature* (1985), and with Donald A. Stanford, James Olney, and Jo Gulledge, *Stories from the Southern Review* (1988). The series editor of the Library of Southern Civilization of Louisiana State University Press, he has served on the editorial board of the Library of America and on various other editorial boards. He is a fellow of the Southern Fellowship of Writers.